D0088873

About My Mother

True Stories of a Horse-Crazy Daughter and
Her Baseball-Obsessed Mother: A Memoir

About My Mother

True Stories of a Horse-Crazy Daughter and
Her Baseball-Obsessed Mother: A Memoir

By Peggy Rowe

Foreword by Mike Rowe

About My Mother
True Stories of a Horse-Crazy Daughter and
Her Baseball-Obsessed Mother: A Memoir

© 2018 Peggy Rowe

Published by Forefront Books.

ISBN: 9781948677165
ISBN: 9781948677172 (eBook)

Acknowledgments

Thanks to friend, editor, and writer Michele "Wojo" Wojciechowski, who read every word of my book, loved it, and told me so—then helped me fix it (www.WojosWorld.com). If there are mistakes, blame them on my last-minute changes. Writers are never finished!

I'm grateful to Rick Bitzelberger for his insight and encouragement and to Mary, Jade, and all the other smart, patient people at mikeroweWORKS for their help.

Thanks to Zest Social Media Solutions for putting the book together. Who knew that it was so complicated?

Last, but not least, thanks to all of Mike's "Little Facebook Friends," who have read my texts and letters and asked me to write a book. See, I do read your entertaining comments! A special thanks to those of you who believe that Mike actually does my writing. You flatter me more than you know!

Dedication

To: My parents, Thelma and Carl Knobel, who were always on the right side of parenting. I once asked my mother why she and Dad didn't have more children. Her response—"The two that we had were perfect"— also happens to be an excellent description of my parents.

To: Janet, a positive influence in my life—kind, smart, ladylike, and always setting a good example—to this day.

To: John, who took it in his stride when I decided that writing was more important than ironing and dusting and fixing breakfast. He's a far, far better husband than he is a writing critic, as he claims to love everything I write. Unless, of course, he's just plain smart.

To: Three sons who remain a priority in my life as well as the beneficiaries of their grandparents' wisdom and love.

Mike, who has taught me much about writing, and who generously shares his fans and his "people" with me. I couldn't have done this without you.

Scott, who has given us a wonderful, loving family, and who tirelessly shares his fascination for sci-fi and fantasy with me. Waiting for your book!

Phil, my karaoke connection, who makes me smile, brings out my mothering instincts, and reminds me what is important in life.

Table of Contents

Foreword

When my mother finally finished the manuscript for her new book, she asked me if I wanted to write the foreword.

"That depends," I said. "Is it any good?"

"Well," she said, "I've sent it off to several publishers. They all say it's terrific!"

"Hey, that's great," I said. "Which publisher did you decide to go with?"

"Oh, they all passed," she said.

"What? Why?"

"They told me a collection of loosely connected stories about a woman no one has ever heard of might be a tough sell in today's highly competitive marketplace."

"I see. So then . . . who exactly is publishing this book of yours?"

"Well, after you write the foreword, you could do it. I thought maybe you could do it!"

Friends of my Facebook page know that my mother has a unique way of getting me to do things. A couple of years ago, after I neglected to return her phone calls in a timely fashion, she posted a short note on my public Facebook page. It read:

Dear Mike,

I assume you're not returning my calls because you're busy making a television show. Or something. But I see that you still have time to chat with your little Facebook friends! Would you prefer to communicate publicly? I'm happy to do so, if it's more convenient for you.

Warmly,
Mom

Obviously, a note like this, posted in front of five million people, prompted some predictable feedback from my loyal fan base.

"Good grief, Mike, call your mother this instant! What's the matter with you?"

"Seriously? You're too busy for your own mother? What kind of person are you?"

Sensing a social media backlash, I called my mother posthaste.

She didn't pick up. I tried again and was sent straight to voicemail.

Clearly, Mom was otherwise engaged, reveling no doubt in the hundreds of sympathetic comments inspired by her passive-aggressive cry for attention. So I left her a message thanking her for turning my fans against me and asking for a return call at her earliest convenience.

What I got instead, a few hours later, was a 1,300-word email that began like this:

"Dear Mike, I was trying to reach you because something happened the other day I *simply had to share...*"

For years, my mother has been sending me true stories she "simply had to share." Some are amusing. Some are touching. Some are laugh-out-loud funny. Well, this was a funny one—a true story that chronicled the mysterious vanishing of her beloved blue purse at the local Walmart and the subsequent drama surrounding its unlikely recovery. She called it "Old Blue," and when I finished reading it, I called my mother again, this time to tell her—for the umpteenth time—that she really should write a book. Once again, my call was sent straight to voicemail. So I hung up, hit the video button on my iPhone, and recorded "Old Blue" from my kitchen table. Then I posted the video on Facebook, jumped into a waiting Uber, and left town for a few days to shoot another episode of something or other.

When I returned, "Old Blue" had been viewed over fifty million times. I'm not even kidding. Fifty. Million. Times. And the feedback was unlike anything I've ever seen. Literally tens of thousands of comments, all begging my mother to write a book.

"Oh my God," they said, "you're the next Erma Bombeck!" "You're the next Nora Ephron!" "You're the next Betty White!"

By the time the dust settled, "Old Blue" had reached well over a hundred million people and caught the eye of several major publishers, all of whom invited my mother to write a book of humorous essays about her relationship with "The Dirty Jobs Guy."

"It's a slam dunk," said one editor. "A no-brainer," said another. "A guaranteed bestseller," said a third.

Mom asked me, "What do you think, Mike? Is a collection of amusing stories about 'The Dirty Jobs Guy' a guaranteed bestseller?"

"Beats me," I said. "But if that's what the big boys say, go for it. Dad will be thrilled. We can all go on a book tour together."

Six months later, I wasn't exactly surprised to receive a 40,000-word email from my mother, broken down into fourteen short stories. Nor was I surprised to discover that each story was packed with warmth and humor and pathos and all the other stuff I expected to find in the stories I knew she'd been working on.

I was, however, surprised to learn that these stories had nothing to do with me, and everything to do with a woman no one has ever heard of—my grandmother. A subject the publishers said would prove to be "a tough sell in today's highly competitive marketplace."

Maybe they're right. Maybe the only way to sell a book these days is to publish something by an established author or rely on some kind of celebrity angle. I don't know. All I can tell you for sure is that my mother doesn't care about "slam dunks," "no-brainers," or "guaranteed bestsellers." She writes what she wants to write about, as these stories conclusively prove. They arrived in my inbox exactly as you see them now, along with a bio, an epilogue, multiple quotes from family members, dozens of photos from days gone by, and everything else a competent printer might require to churn out a book. Everything but a foreword.

Which brings me back to the task at hand. *About My Mother* is the story of a mother and a daughter with absolutely nothing in common—two completely divergent personalities who interacted every single day for the better part of seventy years. The fact that they chose to remain permanent next-door neighbors is still a bit of a mystery, but one that enriched the lives of my two younger brothers and me. Indeed, the resulting sitcom was the bedrock of our upbringing. And Nana was the star of the show. Always.

Judgmental yet loyal, snobby yet kind, haughty yet humble, Nana was a consummate perfectionist and notorious neat freak who sought to keep all those around her scrubbed and tidy and firmly between the lines. She corrected my table manners. She corrected my grammar. She corrected the knot in my tie. Nana corrected the tiniest detail of any casual story that didn't agree precisely with her recollection of the facts. Unless, of course, she was doing the talking. In which case, her exaggerations were boundless.

After I faked my way into the chorus of The Baltimore Opera, Nana began referring to me as "a classically trained musician, fluent in all of the romance languages, and much in demand."

When I was hired to work the midnight shift at QVC, I was suddenly "the number-one salesman in the entire home shopping industry, with an audience as big as David Letterman's."

And when I finally got *Dirty Jobs* on the air—a show that mortified Nana in every way imaginable—she told her friends at church that I was "the biggest television star on cable TV, bravely changing the topography of nonfiction programming."

Nana was what any aspiring writer would call "good material," which is why I thought my mother elected to write about her in the first place. But after reading through these "loosely connected stories about a woman no one has ever heard of," I'm not worried about the fate of my mother's book in "today's competitive marketplace." I think people are hungry for the stories my mother has written, and I can tell you there's a good deal more than gentle humor and fond memories in the pages that follow. There's actual comfort. Comfort for every daughter who ever thought her mother was from another planet. Comfort for every mother who suspected her daughter was switched at birth.

In other words, Mom, I'm glad I ignored your calls back when, and I'm glad you ignored mine. Otherwise, "Old Blue" would have been nothing but a funny story you told me over the telephone, and I wouldn't have had the honor of publishing these fantastic tales that you *"simply had to share."* And that would have been a shame, because when Nana sees this—somewhere from the Great Beyond—I'm pretty sure she'll tell St. Peter I'm "the best publisher of all time!" While down here on earth, I'll be telling the story of the daughter who wrote the book she felt like writing— the "slam dunk, no-brainer, guaranteed bestseller" that kept her mother alive for eternity. Perhaps one day, I can return the favor.

Till then, call me anytime! I promise to pick up...

xoxo,

Mike

Foreword, Part 2

Shortly after I wrote the foreword you've just read, I sent it off to the printer along with my mother's manuscript and a check. In return, I received ten thousand copies of my mother's book, all of which I offered for sale on eBay. Happily, the book sold out immediately, prompting a number of large publishers to reach out with heartfelt congratulations.

Resisting the urge to scream "I told you so," I discussed with these publishers the reasons for the unexpected popularity of Mom's G-rated recollections, and gauged their appetite for a second printing. It appeared to be keen. Meanwhile, actual feedback among those initial ten thousand readers began to pour in, more and more every day. The feedback was not just positive; it was positively effusive. People wanted more. They began sharing stories of their own mothers and daughters and grandmothers. Mom started her own Facebook page, and quickly amassed tens of thousands of fans. Someone called her "America's Grandmother," which may have made her blush, and soon, more publishers came with more offers to write more books. It was pandemonium, but a delightful pandemonium.

Anyway, among those publishers pleasantly surprised by the fact that my mother can actually write was a guy named Jonathan

Merkh who has an imprint called Forefront Books. Thanks to Jonathan and Simon & Schuster, you now hold the second edition of my mother's first book. This one includes five additional stories, along with what I'm told is the only two-part foreword ever published. I sincerely hope you enjoy every word. With luck, I'll be amending this foreword once again, when Simon & Schuster propose a third printing, sometime later this week.

Till then, meet my mother. And my Nana. You're gonna like 'em both. I guarantee it.

Take Me Out to the Ballgame!

It was rush hour in the main aisle of Macy's department store when my ninety-year-old mother rose from her wheelchair and began unbuttoning her blouse.

"Wh-what are you doing, Mom?" I sputtered. "You can't undress here."

"Oh, stop fussing!" she shouted, removing the blouse. "Nobody's interested in an old woman wearing a bra." She pointed across the aisle at a shapeless mannequin in a red-and-white striped bikini. "Look at her! She's wearing less than I am."

It was the kind of logic a child might use—or an older person who was losing her mind. I dropped the handles of the wheelchair and scanned the department for a fitting room. Maybe her behavior was a delayed reaction to the death of my father. You get attached to somebody during seventy years of marriage. Or perhaps congestive heart failure had driven her over the edge.

Suddenly there was a loud commotion behind me. I spun around to see an elderly gentleman—probably distracted by a ninety-year-old woman in a bra—colliding with the mannequin. The mannequin's bald head had crashed to the floor and was rolling about like a bowling ball. Shoppers tripped and toppled over like pins at the end of a bowling alley.

It was all my fault. I should have seen a red flag when Mom pointed ahead like a cavalry officer leading the charge.

"That way, Peggy, and step on it!"

At first I'd thought she wanted to escape the sickening aromas in the perfume aisle, and I was all for that. Then I saw it right in front of us: a display of Baltimore Orioles t-shirts and baseball caps. My mother was drawn to orange and black with the same fervor her neighbors at Oak Crest Retirement Community were drawn to Thursday afternoon bingo.

Her blouse came floating toward me, and I caught it in midair, feeling like Cal Ripken snagging a line drive at Camden Yards. I considered covering my head with it as the commotion around the headless mannequin across the aisle gradually subsided and shoppers turned their attention to the old woman in her underwear.

I jumped in front of my mother and spread my arms as though I were blocking her from shooting a basket.

"Which one of these do you like, honey?" she asked, nonchalantly holding up the orange t-shirts one at a time.

"That one! Quick! Put it on!" I yelled.

She calmly handed me her glasses and pulled the shirt over her head. "Orioles" was in bold black letters across the front. On the back was the Oriole Bird.

"Well," she said, frowning into the mirror. "Orange is not my color—it makes me look washed out." She leaned closer, smoothed her eyebrows, then smiled and said, "But this will be perfect for the Maryland Day celebration tomorrow. I'm going to buy it."

Mom didn't ordinarily go in for trendy fashion. Rather, she had a reputation for being a stylish dresser, and it was a distinction well earned. She had always shopped in "high-end" stores, watching for sales or constructing identical knockoffs on her old black Singer at home. But for her Orioles, she would make the concession. This would be the only garment in her wardrobe with writing on it.

My focus was single-minded as the amused gallery around us watched Mom pick tiny specks of lint from an Orioles t-shirt: I had to derail Gypsy Rose Lee before her encore.

"It looks great, Mom! I know—just wear it home," I said, stuffing her blouse into my purse. "The saleslady will cut off the tags." I looked up to see her staring at me as though I had given birth in the main aisle of Macy's department store.

"Are you crazy? I can't wear this with green pants!" She stripped off the orange-and-black shirt and stood once again in her bra and slacks. On the bright side, it was a lovely bra. But then Mom always *was* dressed for the occasion. On the downside, the skin-tone garment was just that and gave the appearance of, well, skin. Fortunately, it was 2003, before everyone carried a phone with a camera, so our little sideshow didn't go viral.

"Oh, Peggy!" There was disapproval in Mom's voice as she held up the blouse I had just pulled from my purse. "Look at all these wrinkles!"

My mother was complaining about a few wrinkles on a blouse while standing before an audience in her underwear. I had never in all my sixty-seven years spoken disrespectfully to her. Fortunately, she read my expression and put on the wrinkled blouse without further complaint.

Was this the kind of behavior one should expect from a ninety-year-old? I wondered while standing in line at the register. Or, God forbid, was it some form of hereditary dementia? How long before I started removing my clothes in public and embarrassing my children? With my luck, it would happen on a Sunday morning in the choir loft at the front of our church. I would casually put down my music folder and remove my robe and blouse, while the other altos tried to shield me with their music.

Oh well, I thought, smiling to myself as we made our way to the exit. Compared to the trauma she and her beloved Orioles had put me through fifty years earlier, this afternoon was a walk in the park. Besides, things could have been worse. It might have been a display of Orioles underwear.

⚾ ⚾ ⚾ ⚾

When someone asks me what my mother was like, I tell them the truth. I had two mothers—both residing in one body. Mother #1 played contract bridge, listened to opera, and had season tickets to the Baltimore Symphony. She would rather part with her spleen than leave the house in jeans or chew gum in public. Mother #2 was a crazed baseball groupie who shouted obscenities at umpires and threw her underwear at the opposing team. I remember the exact moment *she* came into my life.

I dropped my schoolbooks on a kitchen chair and sniffed the air for the usual breakfast aromas: scrapple, pancakes, stewed apples. "Good old Southern cooking," Dad called it.

But instead of bending over the stove, my mother was bent over the sports section of the morning paper.

"What's for breakfast, Mom?"

Without looking up, she pointed to a box of Corn Flakes on the counter. That's when I saw the orange-and-black chart taped to the refrigerator door.

"What's this?" I asked.

"An Orioles game schedule. Always consult it before you make plans involving me."

"So . . . I don't have to go to the dentist on Thursday?"

"I changed your appointment to Monday. The Orioles don't play on Mondays."

"Hmm . . . looks like I don't have to go to church on Sunday."

Again, without looking up: "Read the schedule, Peggy. Sunday games are in the afternoon."

And that's how it was in 1954. By the time the St. Louis Browns became The Baltimore Orioles, I was in my teens. Just as the colorful stained-glass window was the focal point in our church, the colorful schedule taped to the refrigerator door became the focal point in our home. It didn't help to complain.

"Dad, baseball is controlling our lives! Look, it's five o'clock! Mom hasn't even started supper yet, and I'm supposed to go riding in a half hour."

"Well, maybe *you'd* like to cook something," Dad said.

"I asked her what I should fix," I replied. "She just shushed me and said, 'extra innings.' What are you going to do about it, Dad?"

"Just be patient, hon. The season only lasts until September. Then things will get back to normal. You'll see."

The following evening, my old dog, Topper, and I were lounging on the living room floor watching our only TV and eating popcorn when Mom came breezing in with her sewing basket and changed the channel.

"Hey, that was *I Love Lucy!*"

"Whining is unbecoming a young lady," Mother #1 said. "I'm sorry, but the game's more important."

"Will it be over in an hour? Because *Gunsmoke* comes on, and I can't miss that!"

"Come on. Watch it with me. Not all the games are televised, you know."

During one of the commercials, I changed the channel briefly, and you'd have thought I had jumped up and swung from our treasured crystal chandelier. God forbid we should miss a pitch!

My mother had never shown any interest in sports. I could have understood her obsession if there was a void in her life, but her days were filled running Dad's business, running our church, and running our house—not to mention her busy social schedule.

Not that Orioles games weren't fun. They were, in fact, great family entertainment. Mom was a multitasker long before the term came into vogue. The appearance of the ironing board and laundry basket in the living room signaled more than an imminent ballgame. It was the promise of drama and excitement to rival a three-ring circus. And I had a front row seat!

"Take the pitcher out, Paul! He doesn't have it today. For Pete's sake, what are you waiting for? He's given up three walks and two hits!" Mom screamed, flailing her arms and kicking her legs in the air like a child having a temper tantrum.

"Why are you closing the curtains, Peggy? It's the middle of the day," she'd say.

"Somebody might walk past the window."

"We live in the country, for Pete's sake. I doubt that the horses and rabbits and squirrels are interested in baseball."

Umpires were the enemy. "Get your eyes examined!" she'd yell. "He was safe by a mile!" Then in her very next breath, Mother #1 would reappear. "Peggy, stop slouching. Sit up like a lady."

Once, early on, before he became accustomed to the erratic Orioles fan, Topper was asleep beneath the coffee table at game time. When the Os led off with a home run, Mom squealed like a hyena and Topper shot into the air, hit his head on the table, and knocked himself out cold. "He's just a little groggy," Mom said. "Put a cool, damp towel on his forehead—he'll be himself in no time." After that day, the old whippet was on alert from the minute the ironing board creaked open. Furious barking accompanied Mom's angry shouts at the opposing team and the umps. When things were going especially well for the Os, my "dignified" mother cheered and pranced around the room like the grand marshal in the Macy's Thanksgiving Day Parade. At such times, Topper, his arthritis forgotten, bounded blissfully into the air like a Lipizzaner stallion performing a capriole, his good ear standing tall and his tail waving like the flags atop Memorial Stadium during an Orioles game.

I could only imagine what a stranger coming upon the scene might think as I locked the doors.

Once when I came into the living room from the barn, Orioles' manager Paul Richards was being ejected for going nose-to-nose with a plate umpire who was blind as a bat, according to Mom.

Furious, she reached down into her laundry basket, balled up several pairs of her underpants, and hurled them at the TV screen in protest.

That evening, I took my father aside. "Dad, you need to have a talk with Mom. She's acting like a teenager at a rock concert."

"Oh, hon, she's not all that bad," he said, laughing.

"She threw her underpants at the television!"

"She what?"

"Well, from the laundry basket. But still—what if we had company?" My father had an expression for people who weren't quite normal: "That person is just a half-bubble off," he would say, referring to his tool, the level. I thought he would use it now, but instead he invited me to join him outside for a walk where he came as close as he ever had to admonishing me.

"Your mother has an obsession. You should be able to understand that." He tilted his head toward the stable.

He was referring to my interest in horses, of course. A passion I'd been born with.

"Yeah, but I don't act all weird and embarrass anybody."

Dad shrugged. "How many teenage girls do you know who spend their time shoveling horse manure and galloping through the woods bareback? Some people might think a slumber party in a stable with two horses, a dog, and a chicken is weird."

He had a point. I thought back a couple of nights earlier to when Topper had killed a rat in the tack room, and I carried it by its long tail through the moonlight to the stream. My girlfriends would have shrieked.

"But it's what you love, so it's okay with your mother and me if you want to live in dungarees and smell like a horse. Be patient, hon. Who knows? Maybe we'll learn to love baseball too."

As an afterthought, he added, "And Mom is always at ringside for your horse shows—even when there's a ballgame." I didn't remind him that she had a transistor radio to her ear and cheered loudly at inappropriate times, spooking the horses. But Dad was right. Mom had always tried to be tolerant of my obsession.

"I'll try to be patient," I promised, thinking back to my parents' breakfast conversation that very morning:

Dad: "What time did you finally come to bed, hon? I didn't hear you."

Mom: "It was after midnight. We're on the West Coast this week. You should have seen Clint Courtney. Base runners should know better than to steal with him behind the plate! There was a big rhubarb, and he almost got ejected."

Dad: "I guess that's why they call him Scrap Iron." He loved it when Mom smiled.

Mom: "And he's batting 270. That's not bad. We're in seventh place this morning behind the Washington Senators."

There were only eight teams in our division, but Dad knew better than to intrude on her maniacal sense of optimism. When Mom talked about the grace with which Willie Miranda turned ground balls into outs, or the Bible that manager Paul Richards kept on his office desk, Dad seemed as captivated as when I talked about the new trick I had taught my horse.

Sometimes Dad and I joined Mom for a televised game. Alongside my mother and Topper, we looked like we were drugged. I always checked the schedule on the refrigerator door before inviting friends over.

The first time I saw Mom do her voodoo thing, I was worried we'd have to have her committed. The Os were trailing the White Sox 4–3 in the top of the ninth. We had the bases loaded with two out.

She was standing two feet from the television holding out her left hand. I thought her palm itched because she was rubbing little circles with the fingers of her right hand. Then she closed her eyes, tilted her head heavenward, and began chanting.

We weren't the kind of family that chants. We weren't monks; we were Presbyterians. We didn't speak in tongues or wave our arms about, or shout, "Praise the Lord!"

"Mom, what are you doing? You're scaring me."

"Oh, relax! I'm just putting the Double Whammy on their pitcher. We need base runners." She explained that the little circles represented Orioles rounding the bases.

"Come on, help me! There's strength in numbers."

It was a bunch of mumbo jumbo, and I feared that she was "a *full*-bubble off." Later she giggled like it was all a big joke, but I knew better.

You can keep a passion like my mother's behind closed curtains for only so long. I was fifteen when the "crazy aunt" came down from the attic—and went public.

Mealtime had always been sacred in our home: no television, no radio, no telephone calls. And God help the person who brought a book or magazine to the table. It was a time for conversation—especially before my sister left for college. But since the Orioles came to town, sports radio blared in the background during dinner, and it was "Bob Turley this, Billy Hunter that." Halfway through the meal, Mom would jump from her seat like catcher Clint Courtney springing from a crouch to cut down a runner stealing second and call the station to talk strategy and spout statistics. When her ideas were taken seriously, Dad beamed the way he did when I won a ribbon at a horse show.

Once she answered a difficult trivia question and won a trophy in the form of a unique, smoky-gray glass dish with the Orioles team roster printed in gold. It was displayed on the coffee table until the day my uncle used it to crush out his Camel cigarette. Then it went to live in the china cabinet.

One evening at the beginning of the Orioles second season, the phone rang just as we finished dinner. Mom and I listened as Dad spoke to his friend George whose loud voice carried across the room. George's company, it seemed, owned a coveted open box at Memorial Stadium, home of the Orioles.

"Sometimes we have extra tickets to afternoon games," he said. "Do you think you and Thelma would be interested? I know she's a big fan. Our box is directly behind home plate, and the tickets are free."

Fortunately, Topper was not asleep under the coffee table at the time as my mother's scream was heard by the neighbors on the next farm.

Being in business for himself, Dad arranged to take Mom to the first game. Before I left for school that morning, he winked at me.

"Your mother's walking in tall cotton," he said. In truth, he seemed as excited as Mom, who, for the first time ever, forgot to pack my lunch, check my outfit, and tell me goodbye. At dinner that evening, she was bubbly with details of an Orioles win, while Dad wore his ever-so-patient expression. Two weeks later, he took Mom to a second afternoon game but after that was suddenly too busy with work.

Poor Dad. Seeing my mother dancing in the stands like a showgirl was probably too much for him. And that's when my life took a dark turn.

"I have a surprise. You and I are going to an Orioles game tomorrow afternoon!" Mom exclaimed.

"Sorry, Mom, but I still go to school, remember?"

"This is a special occasion. I'll write a note and pick you up at lunchtime!"

I thought back a couple of weeks when I had asked to skip school in order to prepare for a horse show. You'd have thought I had asked to dye my hair purple. I had to listen to a long lecture on the importance of education.

"You mean . . . watch a baseball game . . . in public?"

"Come on. It'll be fun! I'll buy you a hotdog with everything on it."

And so began the longest summer of my teenage years. That very night I dreamed my mother removed her underpants in front of thousands and threw them at the umpire. As we were escorted from the ballpark with my friends watching, our names were announced over the loud speakers. Of course, that didn't really happen. Oh no. What actually happened was worse.

⚾ ⚾ ⚾ ⚾

On the drive to Memorial Stadium, Mom's knuckles were white against the steering wheel.

"Did I tell you we're playing the Yankees today?" she asked.

"Yes," I answered.

"They're in first place. Don Johnson is pitching for us. He's a righty. Used to be a Yankee so you know he wants a win."

"Mom, you're on the sidewalk!" I said, leaning to my left. "Did you feel that bump? That was the curb! Mom, we're going to end up in a ditch!"

If she was this excited on the way there, I could only imagine how she'd be when we got there. It was like a death march, and the prospect of ending up in a ditch was strangely appealing.

"Gus Triandos is catching today. Sometimes he plays first base. Gus and Don are both big men—six-foot-three."

My attention was drawn to a colorful sign on the side of a building advertising a rodeo at the armory. It featured a trick rider my age. I'd seen a television ad for the rodeo and had been practicing one of her routines on my horse. As Mom prattled on, I closed my eyes and pretended we were on our way to the rodeo right now, instead of. . . .

"Here we are," she said, turning into the stadium parking lot. As we made our way across the blacktop on 33rd Street, she stared at the imposing brick façade. In that very moment, her expression changed, and she looked as if she were about to enter some revered holy place—a cathedral, perhaps. Had we been Catholic, I might have likened her face to St. Bernadette's upon seeing the Virgin Mary at Lourdes. I had probably worried needlessly.

Several strangers were already in the back row of our box as we took our seats at the front.

"Isn't this a beautiful ballpark? Have you ever seen greener grass?" Mom asked, her eyes sparkling like sunlight on the stream that flowed beside our orchard. I was thinking what a nice pasture it would make when she squeezed my arm and pointed ahead.

"Look! The Yankees are taking batting practice and jogging around the outfield." Then she leaned closer and whispered confidentially, "These are the most expensive seats in the ballpark; we won't get hit by foul balls." She pointed to the large, net-like screen behind home plate.

And the umpires won't get hit by flying underwear, I thought as vendors in the aisles shouted, "Get your peanuts! Popcorn! Soda!"

Our box gradually filled—a dozen or so seats—while the odor of cigar smoke wafted over us.

"Hello, Thelma," called George and his wife, Alice.

I turned and waved, and when they asked, "Peggy, are you still riding horses?" I nodded and smiled. I had babysat their three children a couple of times, a job I'd inherited when my sister left for college.

It was soon evident that I had left Mother #1 at the stadium entrance, the way cowboys in the Old West left their six-shooters at the church door.

Laughing at the whacky Orioles fan in our living room was one thing—sitting beside a mother who howled like a coyote when the Orioles got a run was something else. There were no curtains to draw when she screamed, "Get your eyes examined! He was safe by a mile!"

"I'm going to the bathroom," I said when my mother stood up and did a hula dance.

"Are you okay? You just went to the bathroom."

Minutes later I returned to find a hot dog with everything on it. As promised, it was spectacular! My mother, though, was too excited to eat.

I wasn't prepared for the physical pain that came at the top of the fifth inning after lunch. When third baseman Wayne Causey and catcher Gus Triandos had a Yankee in a rundown between third and home, Mom reached over and squeezed my thigh so hard she broke a blood vessel. Before I could say, "Ouch!" Gus tagged him out at the plate, and she pulled me to my feet, wrapped her arms around me, and jumped up and down as though we were sharing a pogo stick.

"Mom! People are staring! Mom, I just ate a hotdog with everything on it, remember!"

She was completely oblivious to the shouts of "Down in front!"

The family lunatic was out of the closet for sure, and I envisioned the end of my babysitting career.

And then came the bottom of the eighth when we were a run behind with two men on—and Mom suddenly extended the dreaded left hand, palm side up.

"Come on, Peggy! We need some runs! It's time for The Double Whammy!"

To a teenager, she may as well have been sacrificing a goat to the home run gods right there in the stands, and I didn't want to be around when the men in white coats dragged her away. So I cringed and hightailed it. When I reached the lower concourse, I heard Mom's voice floating above the crowd.

"Just hit the damn ball!"

⚾ ⚾ ⚾ ⚾

Of course, I lacked the maturity to appreciate my mother's unbridled passion for the Orioles, but I did learn something that summer—besides the fact that sitting next to her required protective gear.

I was the only person embarrassed by my mother's antics. By September, the others in our box were joining in when she danced and cheered.

"Come on, Thelma," they'd shout. "Let's get something going here!" My mother was a flaming cheerleader!

I had no way of knowing that this very same passion that had made my life miserable the summer of 1955 would one day save my mother's life and bring her face to face with her heroes in 2003. But there are a lot of stories to tell before we get to that one.

Home Fires

If you couldn't live on a ranch and be a cowboy, Leslie Avenue was the next best place. There were no mansions or dilapidated shacks on Leslie Avenue—just ordinary houses with doors that were hardly ever locked. It was the 1940s, before cookie-cutter houses were invented, so kids didn't wander into the wrong kitchen at mealtime.

Our brown-shingled two-story was the best house on the block. Not because it was the tallest or the cleanest (although it was). But because it had a front porch big enough for a glider and games of jacks and pickup sticks—or, in my big sister's case, tea parties with paper dolls dressed in the latest fashion. The sturdy railings were perfect for straddling like a horse or for jumping off if I had to escape from a posse. Under the porch was the ultimate hideout—for when my mother was calling me.

The very best feature of Leslie Avenue was the gutter that ran along our side of the road and carried off rainwater and the milky liquid from laundry tubs. On washday or after a storm, it was perfect for leaping over, like the water jump at the Grand National horse race. During a dry spell, it served as an obstacle course for daredevil bicyclists when your mother wasn't watching. Unfortunately, mine always was. Mom had grown up in the country as the oldest of six children and was an expert when it came to taking charge. With her father at sea fishing and her mother preoccupied with a vegetable garden the size of Rhode Island, giving orders came as naturally to Thelma Williams as hauling water from the well and slop buckets to the outhouse.

Nothing irritated my mother more than seeing me have a good time, especially outside in front of the neighbors. Just let me gallop through the yards like a horse, jumping over garbage cans and lawn furniture, and she'd put an end to it as quick as if I had set fire to the laundry on the clothesline.

Another thing my mother couldn't tolerate was idle hands. "Come on, Peggy, I need help washing windows."

"Come on, Peggy, those garden weeds are calling."

"Come on, Peggy, those dishes aren't going to wash themselves."

There was no such thing as climbing a tree while my mother was doing her hummingbird impersonation, flitting from chore to chore, never landing.

Mom was a fan of proverbs. "If a job's worth doing, it's worth doing right!" she preached as I crawled around the floor like Cinderella dusting baseboards and chair legs. She didn't care a fig about child labor laws. If she said it once, she said it a hundred times: "Idle hands are the devil's workshop."

If I was Cinderella, my father was the favored stepsister. He never got yelled at for not putting his things away. He didn't have to listen to, "Do this, do that, get your roller skates off the stairs," every five minutes of his life. Never once did my mother shake her finger at him and say, "Carl, there's a place for everything and everything in its place!" Daddy didn't even have to walk across the bedroom floor to the closet. His personal valet laid his freshly laundered clothes on the bedside chair each morning.

After supper, while my sister, Janet, and I did the dishes, Daddy sat on the living room sofa listening to *Amos 'n' Andy* and

Duffy's Tavern. "Here you go, honey," Mom would say, delivering his hot coffee and apple pie like she was one of those drive-in waitresses.

Dad got to do all the fun stuff, like pushing the noisy lawn mower in the summer and shoveling shiny coal into the furnace in the winter. He was the only one strong enough to open those "blasted" upstairs windows and pry the lids off Mom's canned grape jellies and pickles.

My sister was four years older and stayed busy being charming and getting stars on her papers at school. My mother was forever bragging about her.

"Janet has enough grace and poise for the entire neighborhood," she'd say—whatever that meant.

One evening, my father came home from work late. We were finishing supper when there was a clattering racket in the driveway. Mom jumped up and ran to the window.

"Well, Peggy, the chickens have come home to roost!" I'd heard her say this before so I knew better than to expect a flock of brown hens like the ones in Grandma's yard. "You left your tricycle in the driveway once too often, and your father ran over it with his truck." She shook her finger. "You're in trouble now, young lady. Just you wait until he gets in here."

The thought of my father being angry was as far-fetched as my mother being lazy, but I wasn't one to take chances and scooted beneath the dining room table.

The kitchen door opened and closed. There was whispering, and my father's legs appeared beside the table as he pulled out a chair and sat.

"Somebody left your tricycle in the driveway, Peggy, and I'm afraid I ran over it with my truck. I'm sorry you didn't put it away. Now you won't have anything to ride with your friends."

I scurried from under the table sobbing and buried my face in his shirt. It was dirty and smelly, but I didn't care. Daddy sounded like he was going to cry, and it was my fault.

The tricycle was beyond repair, but I was ready for a bicycle anyway, which I never once left in the driveway!

⚾ ⚾ ⚾ ⚾

Our first family crisis came in 1942. It lasted one whole long, long day and changed our lives for years to come. I was only four at the time and way too busy being an indentured servant to notice the drama surrounding me. But my mother would speak of it often that year and in the years that followed as only she could—with theatrics that left me spellbound.

"Your father is in the war, you know," she would say whenever the topic of WWII came up. "He doesn't carry a gun. His tools are different, but he was drafted just like the soldiers in uniform." Then her eyes would get misty, as she remembered that infamous day—usually while we were doing some quiet chore together, like folding the laundry or shelling butter beans.

"It was a cold Tuesday morning in February," according to Mom. "I had just finished the breakfast dishes when the doorbell rang. I peeked around the curtain, and there was the mailman standing on the porch holding a white envelope. I said to myself, *Now, why doesn't he just put it in the mailbox like he usually does?*

I knew the ending, but always watched wide-eyed like it was a brand-new story I had never heard.

"Then I noticed his expression—like he had just run over our dog. 'Good morning, Joe,' I said, but he handed me the envelope without saying a word. Your father's name was typed, and the return address was Washington, D.C. I stared at it for a long time, then stuck it in that drawer right over there by the stairway."

Then, according to Mom, she scooped me in her arms and cried, which was hard to believe, as she wasn't the crying type.

It was a day filled with dread, apparently. By the time Daddy returned from work and Janet from school, Mom and you-know-who had cleaned our already spotless house from top to bottom and cooked a special dinner. Probably fried chicken, my father's favorite—and steamy, creamy mashed potatoes with a puddle of butter on the top, and a mess of greens like the ones Grandma grew in her garden. The kind that make bones and teeth strong, and, children gag.

"After you and your sister were tucked into bed that night, I took the letter from the drawer and gave it to your father. It was one typewritten page with a beautiful brownish golden eagle at the top."

They read the letter together, and Mom cried what she described as "tears of relief." My father's wartime service would be in a town just fifty miles down the road. Our mother explained it to my sister and me as only she could, being way ahead of her time when it came to "spin."

"President Roosevelt needs Daddy's help in Washington, D.C. Your father will be in charge of keeping the lights on in the nation's capital while our country is at war."

I wasn't sure why the president couldn't turn on his own lights; he must have been frightfully busy. But so it was. While our neighbor's son, Bob, and my Uncle Charles put on uniforms and traveled across the ocean with rifles, my father put on his freshly laundered work clothes (laid out on his bedside chair) and drove down the road to our nation's capital with the tools of a master electrician. There, he kept the lights on in the Navy Yard and The Pentagon, and for all I knew, President Roosevelt's kitchen. We got to see him on Sundays if we were lucky.

Our old next-door neighbor, Mr. Smith, was fond of saying,

"War is hell!" I knew what he meant the day my sandbox was dragged behind the garage to make room for a "victory garden." To compensate for my loss, Mom gave me a small patch of my own and a handful of seeds and showed me how to water and weed my plants. My hard work and patriotism paid off with juicy red "victory melons."

Mrs. Smith hoarded sugar when we couldn't find any to buy. So much for dessert. One day my sister came home from visiting the Smith's daughter with some news that made my mother laugh out loud.

"Guess what? The Smith house is overrun with ants! You should see them. Crawling on the floors and all over the kitchen walls. They were even on the table, and Mr. Smith swears he saw some in the refrigerator. Mrs. Smith is screaming and acting all crazy. Do I have ants in my hair, Mom?" she asked, scratching.

When she stopped laughing, my mother looked through Janet's hair then said something shocking, in her outside voice. "Well, it serves her right!" I knew this was serious because our family didn't talk mean about anybody. I kept an extra close watch on my garden patch in case Mrs. Smith decided to start hoarding watermelons.

While Janet was busy being "Miss Perfect" at school, I was busy being my mother's mule, trudging hundreds of miles a week to the grocery store. Coming home, we'd set down our heavy bags and collapse on the front lawns of strangers.

"Why can't we shop when Daddy's home on Sunday? We could ride in the car."

Instead of reminding me that grocery stores were closed on Sundays, Mom would raise her eyebrows at such an unpatriotic notion and get all dramatic.

"Some children are put on trains and taken far away from their mothers and fathers. They have to live with strangers while the war is on!"

"They're lucky they don't have to walk and lug grocery bags," I said. At times like this, she brought out the big guns.

"Children your age are hiding in bomb shelters at this very minute, afraid that their houses will be blown to bits!"

As feelings of guilt washed over me, she would take a piece of penny candy from her purse for each of us, and we'd be on our way.

When Daddy worked weekends, it was my mother who shoveled the shiny black coal and pushed the noisy lawn mower.

Uncle Charles came to visit and looked so handsome in his dark blue sailor suit and white cap that my mother's eyes filled with tears. Aunt Betty was an Army nurse in far-off places our family had only read about in books. We wrote to them and prayed extra hard at bedtime. My grandmother in Virginia traced their journeys on a map spread across her oak dining room table, nearly ruining it with her tears. On her sideboard was a newspaper article about Uncle Charles's warship. Alongside were two carved wooden elephants Aunt Betty had sent all the way from India.

On one visit home, Aunt Betty brought my mother beautiful brass candlesticks. Our neighbor's son, Bob, brought his mother a beautiful war bride with a funny accent. Mom said she would have been happier with brass candlesticks.

My father's adventures might not have been as exciting as Uncle Charles's, but I was proud when I saw a picture of President Roosevelt in a brightly lit office standing beside an American flag. The only bragging Daddy did was about my mother, who had kept the home fires burning while he was keeping the president's lights on.

Only the Good Stuff

Getting ready for a trip to Grandma Daisy's was like preparing for Christmas. Delicious anticipation!

"We're going down home!" Mom would say with excitement in her voice and a big smile. Dad always worked on *Old Bessie* before we left to make sure she was up to the seven-hour journey.

"She's temperamental," Mom would say, "but your father's good with automobiles. He'll get us there. Your father can do anything!"

And didn't we know it!

Dad called Mom *the organizer* in the family, which was a polite way of saying *the boss*.

"Now, Peggy," she'd say, pointing her finger at me. "You go upstairs and pack some books and games for the trip! I don't want to hear any whining from that back seat!"

She never sounded bossy when she was giving Dad orders, but he always knew what she meant.

"Honey, remember how the children enjoyed that old inner tube you took the last time? That was such a good idea! You even said that it would be nice to have two of them. Remember?" Dad loaded the two inner tubes, and we were on our way.

⚾ ⚾ ⚾ ⚾

Everybody my mother knew had heard about Fleeton. When she wasn't boasting about her children and grandchildren, Mom was singing the praises of the small fishing village where she had spent the first twenty years of her life. She sounded like one of those travel brochures—the kind with pretty illustrations.

"Fleeton is on a peninsula in the Northern Neck of Virginia," she would tell her friends, looking all dreamy-eyed. She'd go on to describe the freshwater ponds and lush gardens that dotted the flat landscape. And then, everybody who hadn't glazed over would hear about the picturesque tidal creeks and saltwater marsh grasses—"so pretty they take your breath away."

Mom claimed that the views from her second-floor windows were "the best in all of Fleeton, and maybe the entire Northern Neck of Virginia."

"I could look from my side bedroom window in the morning and see the sun rise over the mouth of the Great Wicomico River," she'd say. "And, at the end of the day, I could look from my front window and see the same sun setting behind the very same river after it skirted around Fleeton Point." She described Big Fleets Pond at the end of the backyard, Ingram Bay with its sandy shores, and Cockrell Creek that led north to the fish factory and the town of Reedville.

My mother would no more mention the smelly trash and garbage and sewage that was in Big Fleets Pond when she was a girl than she would talk about Grandpop's occasional fondness for whiskey and playing cards for money. Only the good stuff made it into my mother's travel brochure, things like the exquisite osprey, cormorants, ducks, geese, and the ubiquitous seagulls.

With an imagination that rivaled that of Louisa May Alcott

and Emily Brontë, Mom talked about running across the rippling mudflats at low tide—leaving out the part about the seagull droppings that settled into the mud and squished between our toes. She talked about Ingram Bay without mentioning the jellyfish whose long stingers left painful red streaks on our skin; she described the delicate marsh grasses along the shore, leaving out the part about the hungry mosquitos that were big enough to carry off a small child.

Yes, my mother preferred describing the Fleeton she saw from her upstairs windows—where you couldn't see the chicken manure in the side yard or the bees on the clover flowers biding their time until barefoot children came out to play. She could appreciate the beauty of the cocky red roosters strutting through the grass without seeing her mother's bloody chopping block behind the apple tree. There was nary a mention of the snakes that slithered up from the pond into Grandma's lovely garden or the snapping turtles that could make your fingers disappear.

Oh yes, my mother preferred the friendlier, prettier world as seen from her bedroom windows—or, shall we say, as seen from the windows of the bedroom she shared with her four little sisters growing up. I once heard my father describe those upstairs windows as "rose-colored."

⚾ ⚾ ⚾ ⚾

It was a time before electronic games, so we children were left to our own devices on the journey. Janet had her *Nancy Drew Mysteries* and I read horse books. We sometimes counted animals in the fields only to have to bury them when we passed a cemetery.

Deliciously salty moist air blowing through the open car windows, filling our nostrils and making our hair straight, was an unmistakable sign that we were almost there. The final proof was the odor from the fish factory that some people referred to as nauseating. But Grandma Daisy wouldn't hear it. "It's the smell of money," she'd say, as it meant the factory was processing an abundant catch.

In no time at all we were running along the bay shore and floating over gentle saltwater swells on our inner tubes, hoping the sea nettles couldn't reach us. When they did, Mom scraped up handfuls of mud and rubbed the hurt away. When mosquito bites peppered our arms and legs, she made a paste of baking soda and water to treat them.

While Mom was helping Grandma Daisy with gardening or canning or washing clothes in the backyard, Dad taught my sister and me how to fish through holes in the wharf at the end of the road. He laughed loudest of all when we pulled up a perch or a spot.

I told my friends at home about the two-seater outhouse at the end of the path, but I don't think they believed me. There were no words to describe the odor of the slop jar in our bedroom before we carried it to the outhouse in the morning. I even told my friends about the well and the water pump in the backyard, but they weren't impressed.

⚾ ⚾ ⚾ ⚾

"Here it comes!! I shouted when I saw the big mail truck heading down the road to the post office.

"Hold your horses," Dad would say. "We have to eat our lunch first."

Mr. Harding's store was *the* place to go in Fleeton. As in *the only place to go*. It was the highlight of my day, but not because of the neighbors who gathered around the mail slots at the post office end of the store talking about the weather, the fish, or the news. Today, *we* were the news.

"Look who's visiting from Baltimore!" somebody said, as though they just found out. Of course, they had known from the minute our car rounded the bend into Fleeton that Thelma Williams had come home with her family.

Mr. Harding's store was more fun than any carnival (well, except that there were no rides). I could never understand why Janet chose to play with a friend when she could be here. Across from the mail slots was a display case filled with a selection of penny candy that would rival any Woolworth store. Roosting atop the glass case was a red hen, clucking softly. While my father talked with neighbors, I stared at the assortment of candies, deciding how to spend my pennies. When the time came, Mr. Harding slid the glass doors apart and shooed the hen from the countertop.

She made a terrible fuss squawking and flapping her wings and sending up a storm of dust and tiny feathers, some of which settled quietly onto the candy below. It didn't matter. Mr. Harding always blew it off.

After some agonizing decisions, I cupped the small bag of candy in my hand and reached inside. Dad smiled at me as he pulled a list from his shirt pocket. "You're going to save some of that for your sister, right?" It's hard to hear when you're chewing.

And this is the funny part. When Dad pointed to some spools of thread on an upper shelf, Mr. Harding shooed a black and white chicken off of an enormous block of cheese that sat on the floor like a footstool. The chicken was complaining loudly as the storekeeper stepped onto the cheese in his old boots and retrieved two spools of thread. My mother would have complained even louder than the chicken had she been here. I was glad that cheese wasn't on the list.

Grandma raised everything we ate, and our meat was mostly

seafood and ham. She bought her milk down the road.

"It tastes funny," I said, every time I drank it.

"That's because it isn't pasteurized," Grandma would say. "It's pure—right from Miss Douglas's cow!"

Most of all, I treasured those precious hours on the screened-in back porch swing as we watched for Grandpop's fishing boat to come around the lighthouse. Grandma could tell at a glance if he was coming in with a full load.

"Lawsy!" she would exclaim, throwing her hands in the air. "She's low in the water!"

My grumpy grandfather was my least favorite person in the family. But Grandma sounded proud when she described him as the *best captain in the fleet*.

"The other captains gather on our lawn before they go out to ask Charlie where the fish will be running," she said.

I loved my grandmother and the hidden girl within. Her excursions into the past as she shelled butter beans stirred my imagination. When I learned that she'd ridden to school on horseback, I envisioned her galloping at breakneck speed along the country roads beside her brother, Malcolm. Grandma's greatest sorrow was that my Aunt Cornelia had been whisked away by her husband to a faraway land called *Nebraska*. She lifted her apron and wiped away tears whenever she talked about her.

My grandmother's favorite topic was English royalty. She spoke of kings and queens as though she knew them all personally, reciting dates from memory. I heard Dad tell Mom once that Grandma was better than a sleeping pill. More than once I was carried up the steps to bed while she was talking.

Horrific nightmares of an ax-wielding, blood-spattered old lady chasing chickens across the yard, itchy mosquito bites, and painful jellyfish stings were a small price to pay for such idyllic vacations.

Facing the Music

I was eight years old when my mother bought a second-hand piano and started calling our small den the *music room*. She loved referring to the music room as though it were *the conservatory* or *the drawing room*. None of our friends had music rooms.

"Honey," she said to my father after dinner one evening. "Would you help me carry the radio to the music room? That's really where it should be." It was a big Zenith floor model that took up a lot of space. The next day, she brought the record player downstairs from my sister's bedroom and put it beside the radio. Then she talked my father into building some shelves for our records and music books. They were beautiful and sturdy, and, as usual, Dad turned pink when Mom thanked him with a kiss.

The music room was just off the dining room, and before long, our family was introduced to fine dining—with Strauss waltzes playing softly in the background, lacy tablecloths, candles, and linen napkins. Dad even changed from his work clothes and used the nailbrush before dinner. The houses on Leslie Avenue were close together, and some evenings Mom left the curtains open to give the neighbors a glimpse of "civilized dining."

On Saturdays, Janet and I were forced to listen to live performances from The Metropolitan Opera while we did our chores. Mom would read a synopsis from Milton Cross's little opera book beforehand and provide a running commentary as I did the dusting and Janet mopped. Dad hid out in his backyard workshop on Saturdays.

⚾ ⚾ ⚾ ⚾

I knew just where to place the blame for the cultural revolution taking place in our house—squarely on the shoulders of the Overlea Lions Club.

It all started that day my sister and I came home from school and found a strange black truck parked in our driveway. Janet saw it first.

"Look, Peggy," she said, "that truck has our name on it!" Sure enough, printed on the sides was, KNOBEL ELECTRIC COMPANY. Mom was waiting for us on the front porch.

"Your father is an electrical contractor, girls!" she said with a proud smile. "He's a businessman! And I'm his secretary and bookkeeper." Nowadays, her title would be CEO.

Despite Dad's seventh-grade education, Mom had seen great promise in him all those years ago and told us regularly, "There is nothing your father can't do." She didn't have to convince us.

Janet said that, with Mom's ambition and Dad's skill, the business was bound to succeed. And Janet always knew what she was talking about. I hoped she was right. Maybe then we could afford a pony.

Shortly after becoming a businessman, Dad started going to dinner meetings on Thursdays in our church's basement.

"Your father is going to join the Overlea Lions Club. It will be good for our business," Mom told us. "The other members are businessmen too."

Joining the Lions Club expanded my parents' social circle, which had previously consisted of our church family. Their new friends enjoyed entertaining and travel. The wives were the type who went on garden tours and had season subscriptions to the Baltimore Symphony. Dad was active in the club's civic projects, while Mom loved getting dolled up like a movie star and going to dances and banquets. I hardly recognized them when they left the house—Mom in an evening gown and Dad in a bow tie and cufflinks with clean fingernails.

One evening they were invited to a dinner party at the home of a prominent local builder. The next morning at breakfast, Mom's eyes sparkled like the silver service on our buffet as she relived their big night, interrupting herself from time to time to tell me to get my elbows off the table and chew with my mouth closed.

"After dinner their two daughters played beautiful piano duets," she said. "Such delightful girls! Such refined people!"

It was shortly after that evening that my mother bought the piano and christened our small den the *music room*.

In the evening, she would sit at the piano for an impromptu recital. She could only read notes in the treble clef, so, while her right hand played the melody, her left hand free-ranged like the chickens in my grandmother's backyard, pecking the bass keys at random. Houdini had nothing on my mother, who could make an entire family disappear just by sitting on a piano bench.

In December, *The Blue Danube* gave way to *The Nutcracker* and *The Messiah*. As Christmas approached, Mom smiled in a mysterious way. Could it be? Was this the year my prayers would finally be answered? Every year as my family sat at the Christmas Eve service awaiting the arrival of the Messiah, I sat beside them awaiting the arrival of a living, breathing pony. And now, my spirits soared as I pictured Misty of Chincoteague grazing in our backyard. Perhaps the tomboy galloping around the neighborhood had awakened some maternal compassion in my mother.

My excitement peaked on Christmas morning as I followed my sister down the stairs and saw our parents standing beside the tree. I was wearing my cowboy boots and homemade Dale Evans cowgirl skirt in anticipation.

"Merry Christmas!" they said, moving aside so we could see the gifts Santa had left for us.

"Look!" Mom said, pointing to the empty dish on the coffee table where we had left the cookies and carrots for Santa and his reindeer. "I guess they were hungry."

Of course, we were way beyond believing in Santa Claus, but it was part of Christmas. And if they wanted me to believe that it was Santa who had brought my pony, I was more than happy to oblige.

"Look at that! Just a few crumbs left," said Janet, as I flew past her to the kitchen, and threw open the back door.

"Peggy, you're letting the cold air in! Come see what Santa brought," my mother said.

Sadly, maternal compassion took a backseat to culture that Christmas. Instead of finding a furry pony grazing on the back lawn, my sister and I reached into our stockings and found—wait for it—vouchers for piano lessons.

Janet was delirious with joy. "Gee, thanks! Joanne takes piano lessons! I'm going to learn to play as well as she does!"

My father beamed as he always did when Mom was happy. I wanted to jump up and scream at the top of my voice, "If we can afford piano lessons, we can afford a pony!"

But it was Christmas, and the magic of the season hung in the air. Besides, disrespect was not tolerated in our family. There was no negative karma in our home. My sister and I did not argue or fight, and we had never once witnessed a harsh word between our parents. If they disagreed at all, it was in private.

Our piano lessons commenced. With eternal optimism, my mother delivered her two musical ambassadors to the Elmwood Music Studio every Tuesday afternoon. The Overlea Lions Club had a lot to answer for.

At home I practiced roping the trash cans in the backyard to the melodious tones floating from the music room where Janet was practicing her heart out. Tuesday afternoons found me stumbling over the same beginner exercises week after week. Ms. Shiffler's wooden piano bench was a cruel alternative to Misty of Chincoteague.

While my sister played duets with our teacher, I slipped outside and played kickball with the kids on her street.

"I'm no good at playing the piano," I reasoned with my mother. "I hate it! You're wasting Dad's money. Please, can I stop?" Her response was always the same.

"Playing the piano will give you an appreciation for music . . . expose you to culture . . . make you well-rounded . . . blah, blah, blah." So, I plodded on, unaware of the disaster that loomed on the horizon.

Mrs. Shiffler broke it to me gently. "Every spring our students come together for the annual recital, Peggy. They memorize a piece and play it for their parents and guests in a church auditorium."

"No thank you," I said (in my most polite voice).

"Oh, it's lots of fun. We get dressed up, and there are special refreshments. We have a good time."

"I don't think so. But thank you."

"Maybe you'll change your mind. Just in case, we're going to learn this piece for you to play. It's called 'From a Wigwam.' "

I would soon learn that participation in the annual recital was mandatory. It was a ritual of enhanced torture and right up my mother's alley.

She squeezed her black treadle sewing machine into the music room and supervised my practice while she worked on our performance dresses.

My public debut was the stuff of nightmares, thanks to the "no sheet music" rule. Sitting at the piano in my new Singer creation before a packed auditorium, I could scarcely remember my name, much less the opening measure of the piece I'd been forced to memorize. After staring down at my hands until I was cross-eyed, I looked up and saw my teacher. "Here you go, Peggy," she said, smiling sweetly. "Let's just get you started." She placed my fingers on the correct keys. It reminded me of the time my mother couldn't get our car started and Dad put some cables on the battery.

Janet played "The Happy Farmer," and people couldn't believe she'd been playing for only six months.

The abyss of my recital career came the year my mother resorted to psychology. When I finished dressing, she called me in to her bedroom.

"I have something for you, honey," she said, opening her jewelry box. "You know that I'm not superstitious, but I wore these beads last month when I gave a speech to the women of the church. I didn't make one mistake, and everybody complimented me!" She fastened the strand of beads around my neck and turned me to face her. "You'll be good! I know it!"

Before leaving I used a black marker to draw the opening notes of my song on the palms of my hands—just in case the good-luck beads didn't work.

I waited for my turn with that all-too-familiar paralyzing feeling of doom, twisting my mother's necklace until it broke apart and vanished down the front of my dress, one cool bead at a time. Minutes later when my name was called, I meandered to the piano with black marker smeared across my face and new dress. With every step, beads bounced on the linoleum floor around my feet, like hailstones on Grandma's tin roof. Adults laughed while children raced into the aisle chasing down the rolling beads like they were diamonds and rubies. I made it through my piece with a few minor mistakes and as I left the piano, Mrs. Schiffler spit on her handkerchief and wiped off the keys. At least my mother could brag that my performance had been entertaining. The audience *loved* me.

That year Janet's piece was "By a Blue Lagoon." She played the flowing arpeggios and cascading chords like a seasoned musician, looking like an elegantly dressed doll, the kind you're not allowed to play with.

My favorite compliment came from my father, whose dread of recitals equaled mine.

"Hon," he said to me, "I've never heard you play better!" Everybody knew that Dad was tone-deaf.

And still my mother ignored my pleas to stop the lessons, even when I suggested she take piano lessons in my place, which would have been a gift to the entire family.

"Someday you'll thank me," she said.

If only my teacher had been cruel, hitting me over the head with a metronome or screaming at me. But try as I might, I could not dislike this kind, motherly teacher who must have known from the beginning that I was a lost cause when it came to the piano.

Three good things happened that summer: my sister substituted for our church organist and Mom got to sit on the front pew looking proud. The prominent local building contractor and Lions Club member awarded the contract for a sprawling new housing development to the Knobel Electric Company. And last—I was doing my Tarzan impersonation, jumping from the picnic table onto the clothesline pole when it snapped, and I fell to the ground with a concussion and broken clavicle. While on the surface this might not sound like a good thing, my arm was in a sling, and I had four long, glorious weeks before I could play the piano again. So intense was the pain.

⚾ ⚾ ⚾ ⚾

I'm reminded of those lessons often and of my mother's promise that I would thank her someday. She was right, of course, and I think of her when I play the piano at church, especially that Christmas Eve I accompanied a soprano in a *catastrophe-free* performance of "O Holy Night."

My three sons benefited from the music in our home. My insistence that they take piano lessons had paid off. My mother, who lived next door, watched with delight as I hunted them down like little fugitives at lesson time screaming, "Playing the piano will give you an appreciation for music and expose you to culture! Someday you'll thank me!"

Miss Blevins

Miss Blevins had a reputation for being a character—a really fun teacher. It was a well-earned reputation, as there was always laughter radiating from her room. One day when I was taking the scenic route back to my classroom from the lavatory, I ran up the steps to investigate the riotous racket.

Through the small window in the closed door, I could see a boy standing at the front of the room with his arms stretched out to the sides. A closer look revealed that he was standing on one foot like the flamingos at the zoo and balancing a blackboard eraser on his head. It was like a circus act I'd seen, except that this performer wasn't on a tightrope and he looked sad.

That should have been my first clue, but I was naïve and believed Miss Blevins was a special educator like Miss Milton, the librarian. The library was my favorite place in the whole school, and I had read every horse book on the shelves. Miss Milton always gave me a heads-up when a new one arrived. She had seemed as excited as I was about the latest—a complete book of horse care and riding.

"Look, Peggy," she'd said, leafing through the book. "Here's a diagram labeling the parts of the horse—withers, croup, pastern, cannon bone." I didn't have the heart to tell her that I had memorized them years ago, as well as the parts of a saddle and bridle. But the section on the diseases of a horse alone was well worth the purchase price.

When I received a letter saying that I would be in Miss Blevins's fifth-grade classroom, I did cartwheels all the way across our front lawn. Even my mother seemed pleased at my good fortune, which shocked me. She was more a fan of the clichéd, ruler-wielding schoolmarm.

"Maybe a dynamic teacher like Miss Blevins is just what you need!" Then she said something about how a vigorous teacher might awaken my dormant potential. Mom had graduated at the top of her high-school class and knew a lot of big words. She frequently referenced her own teachers when imparting life lessons to my sister and me.

"Mr. Collins might have been strict, but he taught us that there's nothing more important than an education." Or, "Miss Corsa always did say, 'My best students are not necessarily the brightest, but they are the hardest workers!' " Mom had expectations for her two girls. They would behave in a ladylike fashion at all times—and be superior students. Janet excelled in both categories, but it didn't take long for teachers to size me up as "nothing special" when it came to academics. In our house teachers were gods, and that was that—a reality that brought me daily stress. By the end of September, the jury was still out on the plump teacher with the big blue-gray hair and colorful dresses. Perhaps my expectations had been too high. Aside from some intriguing facial tics, she had provided little in the way of entertainment. Maybe it just took her a while to warm up to a new class.

I had blown my big opportunity to impress Miss Blevins the day she sent me on an errand outside of the school. I had never before been singled out for such an honor and felt dizzy at the prospect of escaping the smothering classroom. The kind of attention I usually received was for daydreaming and not finishing my classwork.

"Peggy," she said, "how would you like to run an important errand for me? There's a mailbox down on the corner outside of the post office. You can buy me a stamp, then mail this letter."

A half-hour later, mission accomplished, I returned to the school. "Here you are," I said, handing my teacher the stamp she had asked me to buy. "And I mailed your letter."

In my defense, she never actually told me to put the stamp on the envelope. "What!?" she yelled, looking at me like I was something she had scraped off her shoe. That was my first and last errand for her.

By the end of October, it was painfully evident that Miss Blevins was no Miss Milton, and it was a cruel twist of fate that had landed me in her class. Not only did she give just as much work as other teachers, her methods bordered on sadistic. When she spoke, every eye had better be focused on her action-packed face, or else. If there was a joke, it was always at the expense of one of her subjects, usually some clueless boy. Old Twitchy Bat (my affectionate name for her, though I never voiced it aloud, especially at home) had no use for boys. If someone didn't complete a homework assignment, for instance, she would place him in front of the class and perform a stand-up routine for her captive audience.

"And just how did you spend your time last night, instead of doing homework, Mr. Dunce? Judging from the dirt behind your ears, I'd say you weren't taking a bath. Judging from the wrinkles in your shirt, I doubt that you were ironing."

Two girls in our class enjoyed *most favored students* status. "Teacher's pets," we called them. They had the privilege of grading papers and running errands while the rest of us were chained to our desks. From time to time, Miss Blevins would exchange looks with the girls as though they were privy to some inside joke.

Ruthie and Gloria were on duty whenever Old Twitchy Bat took a break, presumably to hang by her heels in a darkened cloakroom. With an excess of self-confidence, they stood at the front of the room rolling chalk between their palms while their beady eyes darted around the room in search of some minor rule infraction—like breathing or blinking. If your name appeared in the dreaded box in the corner of the blackboard, you could kiss recess goodbye. I had to be extra careful, as the two toadies were my favorite targets in Greek dodgeball and delighted in keeping my wicked arm off the playground.

At the other end of the spectrum were the unfortunate victims Miss Blevins tortured for amusement. When she blinked her eyes rapidly while jutting her jaw forward and pressing her lips together in a cruel grin, some poor sucker was headed for the trash can for sure. Once wedged inside, he sat bent like a pretzel with his feet dangling over the side, and his knees poking his chin. The trash can was Miss Blevins's version of the stocks I had seen on a family visit to Williamsburg, Virginia, the previous summer. (One of the educational vacations my mother preferred over a trip to the ocean or an amusement park.) Lawbreaking colonists who were put into the stocks were subjected to ridicule and abuse from the decent, law-abiding citizens. The trash can punishment was rarely meted out in anger, more so for its entertainment value. If the can was already occupied when you misbehaved, or if you were too chubby, you were relegated to solitary beneath the tyrant's desk beside her chunky calves until you learned your lesson.

I had stupidly complained about her brutal tactics at dinner one evening. Big mistake!

"I didn't have Miss Blevins," said Janet, now a sophisticated high-school freshman, "but I heard stories about her." Dad gave me a sympathetic look, but naturally, my mother missed the point entirely, and treated me to a flash of anger.

"I'd better never hear that your behavior resulted in a trip to that trash can, young lady!"

Of course, I joined my classmates in laughing at our teacher's shenanigans, relieved not to be the one in her crosshairs. It was a diversion from classwork, after all. Until that fateful Friday afternoon in late April when I became her target.

I was sitting in class, scarcely breathing and avoiding eye contact with the snitch du jour, when Miss Blevins appeared in the doorway with the teacher from next door.

She was itching for a fight, and seeing that the box in the corner of the blackboard was empty, unleashed her fury.

"This class has been a colossal disappointment this year!" she told the other teacher.

Without warning, she picked up a blackboard eraser and hurled it with uncanny accuracy at Teddy Zimmer's head. As the laughter subsided, she turned her piercing gaze on me, the way lions at the zoo stare at a piece of meat at feeding time. I expected an eraser to come hurling through the air at any minute and was toying with the idea of throwing it back at her—until I envisioned my disapproving mother coming into the office for a conference. Suddenly I heard my name.

"Take Peggy Knobel, for example. She used to be a nice little girl. Stand up, Peggy, so Miss Price can see what a lazy student looks like."

"I taught her sister. She was a model scholar," said the teacher from next door, making little *tsk, tsk* sounds and shaking her head as though I had set fire to the flag in the corner of the classroom.

The tyrant's face was twitching at warp speed like jet engines revving up before takeoff. Tears stung my eyes as classmates stared. Gloria leaned across the aisle and whispered loudly, "Miss Blevins told you to stand up!"

There was a red mark on her upper arm from my accurate

throw in Greek Dodge at recess, and, if my situation hadn't been so dire, I might have pointed it out to her.

"Yeah!" Ruthie chimed in.

That's when something snapped, and my inner rebel exploded big time. Clenching my fists and gritting my teeth, I jumped up and raced for the door, wondering briefly if my dormant potential had awakened. Probably not what my mother had in mind.

Just like the Red Sea had parted before Moses, the two educators jumped aside as I flew through the doorway and down the steps. The tyrant's furious voice echoed in the stairwell.

"Peggy Knobel, where do you think you're going? You come back here, young lady! Did you hear?" The heavy door slammed behind me.

I dashed blindly across the playground and through the Greek dodgeball court where I had been the hero at recess. At the end of the driveway, I slowed down and summoned the courage to look back, fearful of seeing big blue-gray hair and a purple dress in hot pursuit, her thick thighs rubbing together like a cricket's legs. The coast was clear, and my adrenaline was still pumping when I turned onto Fullerton Avenue and proceeded to the corner of Linhigh Avenue.

I jumped the white picket fence beside the store owned by the Bakers and came to a screeching halt. What in the world was I doing?! I was taking my usual route home. The home where my mother was ironing and listening to her favorite radio show, *Life Can Be Beautiful*. What would I tell her? "The teacher goddess called me lazy!?" I looked back towards the school, then towards Leslie Avenue, trying to think. I could say that I was sick. But eventually, the phone would ring.

To my right, at the end of the block, was our church. Huh! Where was God now? Religion was so overrated!

Shoulders slumped, I turned around and retraced my steps,

wondering if the day would ever come when I didn't care about my mother's disapproval.

Minutes later I entered the side door of Fullerton School praying that the call had not been made. I took the longer route to my room, down the first-floor hallway past the library.

Miss Milton smiled at me and waved through the open door, unaware that she was giving comfort to a fugitive. The cheerful afternoon sunlight poured through the long windows behind her, making a halo around her head and shining onto a pot of yellow spring daisies on her desk.

I tore myself away from the peaceful scene and crept down the dark, dismal hallway, tiptoeing past the faculty room. At that very moment, the door to the principal's office swung wide, and I stood face to face with none other than Old Twitchy Bat.

She looked at me for a second, then called over her shoulder, "She's back!" Her eyes were little slits when she turned back to me. "Mr. Rush wants to see you—now!" Her words were spewed with enough venom to wither an entire field of yellow spring daisies. Her expression hinted that if I survived my visit with the principal, she would see to it that I'd be bypassing the trash can and proceeding directly to the incinerator.

I'd never met our principal personally, but his crewcut and bow tie made him seem less menacing than he probably would have liked. I can picture it like a photograph, frozen in time and, seventy years later, still in focus. I see that aggrieved tyrant perched stiffly on the edge of her chair as though rigor mortis had set in and the boy-principal leaning against the corner of his desk. The thought of my mother walking through the office door was enough to give me the dry heaves, and I slapped my hand over my mouth.

"Your teacher tells me you left school without permission, Peggy. We were worried. Where have you been?"

The smell of coffee filled the small room and, while that might not sound like a good thing for the dry heaves, it reminded me of my father—my kind, nonjudgmental father. Compared to his own exploits at this very school, my discretion was akin to burping aloud during the Sunday sermon. When he was my age, Dad had been suspended for smoking in the outhouse. Instead of giving his parents the principal's note, he'd hidden out at a nearby stream for three days during school, uncovering a clandestine moonshine operation in the woods. I treasured his Tom Sawyer like adventures and begged to hear them over and over when we were alone. Tales of disobedience were not the sort of stories my mother enjoyed.

"Well?" the boy-principal asked, folding his arms and trying to look intimidating. He could have taken lessons from my mother.

"I went home," I said, looking up at him. "That is, I *started* for home."

They were hanging on my every word, as though I were a famous orator and they'd bought a ticket to my performance.

"I came back because . . ." I shrugged. Miss Blevins blew her nose, putting on a show of concern for me, and in a stroke of genius I blurted, "because I knew you'd be worried."

Mr. Rush's face softened as he placed his hand on a folder on his desk. "I took a few minutes to look over your records. You've never done anything like this before. What happened today, Peggy?" He sounded like my father, and I sensed an ally—as though Miss Blevins was the one in trouble.

The sound of clicking typewriter keys came from the adjoining office, filling the silence.

"Your teacher and I are waiting. What happened today?"

Taking a page from my teacher's playbook, I sniffed and blinked and my voice might have quivered the tiniest bit. "M-miss Blevins knows why I left."

Playing her part to the hilt, the old bat looked at me, bewildered and innocent, and shook her head. I was rotten to the core, of course, but Miss Blevins was no teacher of the year herself. I had no choice but to throw her under the school bus.

"You told Miss Price I was lazy and not nice and ordered me to stand up so everybody could make fun of me." I shrugged. "I-I didn't want to sit in the trash can . . . or . . . or on the floor under your desk."

My teacher seemed to shrink in size, pressed her lips together, and reached for another tissue.

"What you did was dangerous, Peggy, and against school rules!" said Mr. Rush. "You are never to leave this school again without permission! Is that understood?"

"Yes sir."

"Ordinarily, I would invite your parents in for a conference, but if you give me your word that this will never happen again, that won't be necessary."

"Yes sir. Uh, no sir."

"We'll just keep this between us then." He looked at the clock and jotted a message on a notepad the way a doctor does when he's finished with you.

"Dismissal is in an hour. You can help Miss Milton in the library while I have a chat with your teacher. Give her this note, and we'll all have a fresh start on Monday morning. I'm sure you've learned a valuable lesson today."

I headed for my punishment, being careful not to skip until the door closed behind me. I had learned a lesson that day— teachers weren't perfect. Not that I could tell that to my mother.

I suspected that I wasn't the only one to learn a lesson, as trash cans were used solely for trash after that day, and the space beneath Miss Blevins's desk was reserved for her pudgy legs alone. I became the invisible student, all-but-ignored by my teacher, who was busy checking off the days until her retirement.

Ahead of Her Time

When I was a little girl, most of my friends' mothers didn't even know how to drive a car. And those who did drove only as far as the grocery store or to church. Sometimes on a rainy day, my friend Laverne's mother would take "the machine," as she called it, out of the garage and drive us the half-mile to Fullerton School. It was a big deal! That's what made a trip I took with my mom in 1948 so remarkable.

Grandma could cry *at the drop of a hat,* as Dad once put it. She would have made a wonderful actress, as they have to cry a lot. Grandma could even cry when she was laughing—kind of a half-cry, half-laugh. And "cry" is exactly what she did whenever the topic of Aunt Cornelia in far-off Nebraska came up.

It made my mother sad, too, so when I was ten years old, she did something unheard of for a woman of that time.

She put my grandmother, my sister, and me in our old jalopy and drove 1,000 miles—halfway across the country to Omaha, Nebraska—without a man.

⚾ ⚾ ⚾ ⚾

Before we left, my father went over our car, *Old Bessie,* with a fine-tooth comb and pronounced her roadworthy. Mom left Dad enough meals to feed "our whole congregation" while we were gone.

Janet sat on the front seat beside our mother with a big map spread across her lap, while I sat on the backseat beside Grandma Daisy. I kept my eyes peeled for cowboys and wild horses as we crept westward through dozens of small towns that all looked the same. There were no golden arches or smartphones in 1948. We shopped at grocery stores and treated ourselves to the occasional gourmet meal at Woolworth lunch counters. After lunch we gave Mom back massages, and sometimes she took a short nap. We stopped driving well before dark and spent nights in tourist homes where I saw endless fields of corn and wheat in my sleep. Mom called Dad every night on pay phones.

Seatbelts, like efficient interstate highways and budget motels, were things of the future. The afternoon Mom drove onto a deeply rutted shoulder, my head hit the roof and Grandma bounced off the back seat onto the floor. When the car came to a stop, we all giggled, and my grandmother launched into a story about the day her father's horse bolted and she and her brother, Malcolm, were thrown to the carriage floor.

On the fourth day, we arrived in Omaha. Grandma, Mom, and Aunt Cornelia—Aunt Nealie to us—talked and laughed nonstop while Janet and I got acquainted with our two-year-old cousin. There were games and puzzles and drives to my uncle's family farm, which had corn and wheat and big farm machinery, but not a single horse. As planned, a week into our visit, my father took a train to Omaha to reclaim his family. My mother was so giddy you'd have thought she was sixteen and getting ready for her first date. As we left the house for the train station to pick Dad up, she paused at the door, looked in the mirror, and shook her head.

"Carl has seen me in this old thing a hundred times."

Aunt Nealie laughed.

"Thelma, Carl would think you were beautiful if you were wearing a burlap bag." She took Mom into her bedroom and gave her a brand-new blouse that she had never worn. Imagine, an *old woman* of thirty-five caring how she looked to the man she'd been married to for fifteen years.

On the way home, Grandma sat on the back seat between Janet and me while Dad and Mom sat close together up front and talked and giggled all flirty-like. Friends couldn't believe that my mother had driven halfway across the United States without a man. Her family wasn't surprised at all.

I couldn't believe that we had driven halfway across the United States without seeing one horse.

The Christmas Conspiracy

In our house, Christmas revolved around three people: Jesus, Santa Claus, and my mother—not necessarily in that order. Mom loved Christmas. All of it. At no other season of the year were her micro-managing skills more in evidence. She presided over Christmas the way a teacher presides over her classroom—planning, giving assignments, and supervising.

"Now, girls, remember, we place one icicle at a time very carefully over the branch, like this! Not two, not three, but one."

"We'll never finish that way!" we protested. "Look, it says there are one thousand icicles in the box. Why can't we just throw a handful?" I asked that question every year, even though I knew the answer.

"Absolutely not! One at a time, just so. It looks neater that way."

"Christmas morning will be here, and we'll still be hanging icicles!" I complained to no avail.

Dad strung the outdoor lights—under supervision, of course. Mom wasn't about to leave anything to chance.

"They look nice, honey," she'd say. "But there are too many blue lights on this side of the porch. We could use some yellow and red lights over here."

Dad pretty much had free rein when it came to the

Christmas garden, as long as certain landmarks were in the right place. The church had to be precisely in the center of the village, just as it was at the center of our lives. And the papier-mâché mountain had to straddle the tracks at the end of the garden. The effect of the train's headlight bursting through the dark tunnel as it rounded the curve had a dramatic effect, especially when the room was dark.

Running the train was a man's job. One year I goaded my father into racing our electric train faster and faster around the Christmas garden until it jumped the track and crashed into the manger. I laughed hysterically when Baby Jesus was catapulted into the air over a white picket fence and splashed into the shallow duck pond. I laughed again at my father's sheepish grin when Mom raised her eyebrows in disapproval.

My father might have been merely a supporting player at this season of the year, but he was the best. The Christmas he built sturdy bookcases for my sister and me, Janet couldn't wait to arrange her *Nancy Drew Mysteries* and the set of orange *Childcraft* books that were our go-to source for any and all questions. I kept my horse books in mine, along with a collection of horse figurines I had won at the annual Lions Club carnivals. The Christmas morning I received a shiny green bicycle from Santa Claus, I pretended not to notice the matching green paint on Dad's hands. It merely confirmed my suspicions.

⚾ ⚾ ⚾ ⚾

My mother was famous for her sugar cookies. Every year Dad held one up to the light and said the same thing. "These are rolled so thin, I could read the newspaper through them, hon."

It wasn't true, but it always made Mom laugh and say, "Oh,

Carl." At lunch, he'd wink and slide his coffee cup closer to me. We shared a passion for dunking sugar cookies. Mom looked the other way on such occasions. She was ahead of her time when it came to the concept of *picking her battles*. Lucky for me, my chair was next to my father's. He never told me to get my elbows off the table or to chew with my mouth closed.

My favorite part of Christmas, other than the presents, was the Christmas Eve candlelight service, a time of magic when my sister and I huddled between our parents in our new homemade outfits, with approximately one-hundred pounds of lace and ruffles. The true miracle of Christmas was that we could sit up straight under the weight. The best part of the service came after the preacher read the Christmas story from the Bible and the choir sang.

One at a time the lights were extinguished, until we were plunged into total darkness, a perfect time for my favorite prayer. "Please, God, can I have a pony? I promise I'll take care of him and love him."

Once I had said to my mother, "If you really loved me, you'd buy me a pony." She responded that children who get everything they want are unhappy children. By Mom's standards, I had a happy childhood indeed. After the preacher talked for a minute in the darkness, candles were lit, and the sanctuary was bathed in a soft yellow magic glow. That was a good thing except that peoples' faces looked all spooky behind the flickering lights, like skulls in a scary movie.

⚾ ⚾ ⚾ ⚾

Then came the weird part of Christmas—the part that was unique to our family. I knew early on that every gift beneath the tree had been selected and purchased by my mother. She had even purchased the gifts my father, sister, and I gave to her.

"I know what I need," she'd say, weeks before Christmas. "I may as well just buy it myself. You can wrap it." She also knew what my father needed, as well as what my sister and I needed.

When Mom opened her gifts on Christmas morning, she *oohed* and *aahed* over our impeccable taste. "Oh, I love it," she'd say, looking surprised. "It's exactly what I wanted."

My biggest surprise on Christmas morning was the gifts *I* had given to my family. I watched with as much suspense as my sister as she unwrapped her present from me.

This arrangement was fine with my father, who would rather listen to my mother play an entire concerto on the piano than to go into a store. Dad didn't shop—ever! Mom bought his clothes and even his shoes, sometimes returning to the store three times for the perfect fit.

The truth is that, when it came to gifts, Christmas in our house was a conspiracy. As the years went on, it became even more so . . . with one exception. The Christmas before Janet left for college, she took me aside.

"Peggy, do you think you can keep a secret?" she asked.

I couldn't believe it. My heart felt like the thundering hoof beats of the great horse Silver. At the age of sixteen, Janet was actually going to confide in me—a first. She was treating me like a friend instead of the annoying twelve-year-old sister I was. I smiled. "Sure, I can keep a secret."

"How would you like to give Mom and Dad a surprise gift for Christmas this year?"

"Uh, Mom doesn't like surprises."

"I guarantee you, she and Dad will love this one! I've made arrangements with a photographer to take our picture. And I have enough money for a pretty frame." Janet had a part-time job at Woolworth; naturally, then, she was independently wealthy.

So thanks to my grown-up sister, my mother got to open a gift on Christmas morning that she had not purchased. Janet had been right, of course. Our parents looked at the photograph together and were too overwhelmed to speak. I was afraid Mom might cry, but she started running around the room, setting the picture here, and then there. In the end, our photograph went to live on the lovely old mahogany drop-leaf table across from the front door so that visitors would see it first thing.

The following year, with my sister away at college, Dad came to me in early December. "Hon, could you find out what your mother wants for Christmas? I'll give you some money, and you can pick it out for me. I'd give anything to see the look on her face when she finds a gift under the tree that's really from me."

The following morning at breakfast I put out some feelers.

"You've had that old bathrobe as long as I can remember, Mom."

Her eyes narrowed. "Did your father ask you to buy me a new robe for Christmas?"

"Well, no . . ." I lied, avoiding her eyes.

"Because if he did, I'd rather buy it myself. I know what I like and where to get it on sale."

"But, he wants to surprise you," I said, feeling miserably disloyal.

"Oh, I'll be surprised, all right. Just give me Dad's money, and I'll buy the robe. You can wrap it. It'll be nicer than any robe you can find at Woolworth or the drug store."

She was wrong. I'd seen a pretty bathrobe at Woolworth that she would have loved. It was red and furry with a picture of the American flag on the back. We could have recited the pledge every morning while Mom flipped pancakes.

That was the year I began doing Dad's Christmas shopping for Mom. Or so he believed. Long before he even thought about

Mom's gift, she had already purchased and hidden it. She would give it to me, I would give her Dad's money, wrap the gift, then give it to Dad so that he could surprise her on Christmas morning. It was as simple as that. Our deception took a detour the year Dad got specific.

"Your mother likes pink," he said. "I want to give her a pink sweater."

"Pink?! I haven't bought anything pink since you were a baby!" she said when I told her. The next day she returned the pocketbook she had already purchased.

That Christmas morning, we were treated to an Oscar-worthy performance as Mom modeled her gift. Dad's face turned as pink as the sweater when Mom kissed his cheek.

Thrilled at having surprised the love of his life once again, he winked at me. "You always seem to know what your mother likes. Do you mind doing my shopping?"

"It's no trouble at all," I assured him. "Really, Dad. Christmas shopping is one of those family traditions I'll always remember."

And that was the truth!

Just the Two of Us

For the first seven years of my life, my mother suffered from a condition called *intermittent deafness*. It came and went, kind of like those intermittent showers the weatherman warned about on the radio. I finally put two and two together after I heard a story about people who went blind from looking at the sun too often. I became convinced my mother went deaf from hearing the word *pony* too often.

So for my seventh birthday, I changed my strategy.

"Well, if I can't have a *you know what*, can I at least have a cowboy hat? That prairie sun is awful hard on a cowboy's eyes, you know."

Instead of admonishing, *"Little ladies do not wear cowboy hats!"* she lowered her head, stared at me for a minute, heaved a big sigh, and flopped backwards onto the sofa, gazing up at the ceiling as if she were . . . well . . . you know . . . *dead*.

I've never known for certain if *mother-love* triumphed or if Mom decided she could survive with just one refined young lady for the time being. Or perhaps she'd convinced herself I was just going through a phase that would soon pass. Either way, my mother had seen her dream of a second refined young lady gallop out of sight, lace on her socks and a floppy bow in her hair. It was time to adjust her expectations, just as I had. In reality, she was trying to come to terms with having given birth to a misfit.

Seconds later, she blinked, looked at me, and, sounding as old as my grandmother, asked, "What color?"

It was a carpe diem moment for sure.

"Tan like Roy Rogers," I said in my outside voice. "And no lace or bows, please! Just a plain old cowboy hat!"

The hat was a mere slippery slope to the pair of pointy-toed cowboy boots for Christmas. Mom knew a thing or two about economy so they were three sizes larger than my feet. My big sister could have worn them easily—which was as likely to happen as my waking up and finding a pony tied to my bedpost. Mom looked apologetic as she balled up the morning newspaper and wedged it into the toes.

I cuddled the boots to my chest and rubbed the soft leather against my cheek. "If I get bored sitting around the campfire while I'm on a cattle drive, I can take out the paper and read the funnies." I could tell by Mom's smile that, had we been a family of huggers, this would be one of those occasions.

In no time at all I learned to walk in my new boots without bumping into walls. And chairs. And doors. I *never* outgrew them. Mom was so smart. And who'd have guessed that fingers so adept at ruffles and lace could sew a Dale Evans cowgirl skirt—with fringe?

The cap pistol was a harder sell and the final piece of the puzzle that nailed down my reputation as "neighborhood misfit." At least Mom could brag that her daughter was the *best-dressed* misfit in the neighborhood.

One afternoon in late summer, after my dog Topper and I had rounded up stray dogies from a canyon (the alley behind the house), I straddled the sturdy pole that supported the backyard grapevines to enjoy some ripe fruit. And presto! My virtual pony was born!

After she recovered from the shock of my purple legs, Mom snipped the ripe bunches of Concord grapes from the vines and put them in a pot for jelly. Then she made a trip to the steamy attic and returned with a thick old cushion and some clothesline. With reins and a soft saddle, I mounted my grapevine steed and headed for the high country.

Neighbors who'd grown accustomed to the two-legged horse leaping over their hedges and birdbaths now shook their heads at the dysfunctional kid perched atop the grapevines for hours at a time. I looked like some oversized ornament on a weathervane decked out in a ten-gallon hat and enormous pointy-toed boots. If they'd been close enough, they could have heard me singing "Tumbling Tumbleweeds" and firing off the occasional round from my cap pistol.

Had they only known of my exciting adventures! I expect Mom did, because, where some mothers would have sought counseling, mine gave my pony a name: *Cordie*, after Concord grapes. She bought me horse books, and together we read *Black Beauty* and my all-time favorite, *Misty of Chincoteague*.

My mother would continue to nourish my obsession, taking me to the movies to see *My Friend Flicka* and to horse shows at the state fair. But nothing was as memorable as the wild pony roundup in Chincoteague, Virginia—a trip that would reveal my mother's bold nature like nothing else. Janet practically got down on her knees and begged to stay home and keep house for Dad. Poor Janet! She didn't know what she was missing.

Our first stop in Chincoteague was at a motel of sorts, where my mother had an unpleasant encounter with the owner. I don't recall the exact words, but I do remember staring down at my cowboy boots and inching toward the door. It went something like this:

"We have one vacancy. That'll be $75."

"What?!" My mother was using her outside voice—something I'd always been discouraged from doing when I was inside. She slapped her right hand over her heart and fluttered it as though the news had given her a major coronary.

"I want to rent a room for the night. I don't want to buy the building!"

"Take it or leave it."

"Shame on you, taking advantage of a woman and child! I have a good mind to report you!" There was more, but it was hard to hear from the sidewalk. Instead of calling the government authorities, she drove around town looking for another place to spend the night. Still unsuccessful at sunset, we pulled up to the volunteer fire department.

"I'll wait in the car," I said.

"Oh no, you won't. I need you with me."

Inside my mother put her arm around me and explained to the firemen that we were far from home with no place to stay. It was Bethlehem all over again, only instead of a crude stable, we spent the night in our Chevy station wagon, safely parked outside the front door of the firehouse—*complete with complimentary donuts and bathroom privileges*. It occurred to me that, if Joseph had had my mother along, the Christmas story would have played out much differently.

There were no shepherds or kings to stand guard, just some firemen nearby. But just like the Star of Bethlehem shone down on the little stable, the engine house light shone down on our Chevy station wagon with the wooden side panels. Slathered in slippery bug repellent, we locked the doors, cracked the windows, and were asleep in no time.

The next day, we sat in a boat as *saltwater cowboys* swam dozens of ponies across the Assateague Channel. Dozens of beautiful, coura-geous ponies—and I couldn't even have *one*. They came so close, I fantasized about jumping from the rail of the boat onto the back of a pony that looked just like Misty's spotted mother, Phantom.

Afterwards Mom drove us to the Beebe ranch featured in *Misty of Chincoteague*. She parked at the curb and we stared for a long time. Suddenly she said, "Come on," and got out of the car.

"Where are you going?" I protested. "We can't go in there! We don't know these people!"

"Of *course* we do. We bought their book and read it, didn't we?" She looked at me and shrugged. "Nothing ventured, nothing gained. Come on. We've come this far." And then, bold as brass, she walked right up to the door like she was a long-lost relative. My mother had more nerve than the snakes that slithered toward Grandma Daisy while she was swinging her garden hoe. When a friendly Mr. Beebe came outside and spoke with us, Mom introduced herself.

"We're practically neighbors," she said, and she proceeded to tell him about growing up in Fleeton, Virginia.

Yes, he had heard of Fleeton, and yes, he might even have heard of Captain Charles Williams, my grandfather. Minutes later, he gave me a big smile and said, "Thank you for coming and for saying hello to me. I hope you and your little girl have a good visit."

"What a nice man!" she said as we returned to our car.

I could tell he had been impressed by my cowboy boots and Dale Evans skirt.

That evening, we went to the carnival grounds and watched farriers trim the ponies' hooves. I was shocked at how grotesque and misshapen they were. A cowboy explained that living on the wet marshland caused the hooves to be soft and easily molded. I had learned from my reading that their large bellies were a result of eating the salty marsh grasses.

My mother's favorite part of the trip was the food at the carnival grounds. "It's the best in the world," she said. "And these country cooks know what they're doing." She had oyster fritters and a soft crab and sliced red tomatoes. I had corn on the cob and a hush puppy (that didn't look at all like a dog).

That night, as we slept in front of the fire department with a sheet pulled up to our necks, a deafening siren screamed in the wee hours and sent us bolting upright. In a Kumbaya moment, with our faces all shiny and slippery and our eyes bugged out, we held on to each other, shaking, then laughing hysterically as engines raced from the firehouse just feet away.

"Were you scared?" I asked when it was quiet again and we were lying in our coffinlike bed on wheels.

Mom thought for a moment. "Not as scared as I was the night I almost died of appendicitis. The doctor carried me through the fog to a boat that took us to Baltimore. I had a high fever and terrible pain in my side."

I leaned on my elbows and watched Mom's face intently in the light from the firehouse. I had heard the story before, of course, but nobody told a story quite like my mother. It was a little different each time. It was hard to tell for sure because of all the gooey bug repellent, but I was almost certain there were tears on her cheeks.

"Were you afraid because you thought you would die?" I asked.

"I was afraid because Mama wasn't there. She'd just had my baby sister. And how could she manage without me if I didn't come back?"

I lay back down and snuggled against my mother's side. She put her arm around my shoulder, and I felt like the luckiest person in the world. Minutes later we drifted back to sleep with mosquitos buzzing around our ears. Just the two of us.

The next morning at the pony auction, I almost pointed out again that the foals were small enough to fit in the back of our station wagon, but I changed my mind.

We were halfway home that afternoon when a police car with flashing lights pulled us over. What followed, was a performance deserving of an award.

"What's the matter, Officer? Is there something wrong with my car?"

"Yes ma'am, it was going too fast—45 in a 30-mile-an-hour zone. Your license and registration, please."

"Me? Speeding? You're mistaken. I've been driving since I was twelve years old. I've never gotten a ticket—never even been pulled over."

"Your registration, please, ma'am."

My mother put her hand over her heart and began breathing faster and coughing. "I don't feel well. This has never happened to me before!"

"You'll be all right, ma'am."

I took a card from an envelope in the glove compartment, handed it to the policeman, and slid lower in my seat.

With her hand still over her heart, she whispered, "Are you sure? Because I've never..."

"I'm sure, Mrs. Knobel," he said, writing in a book. "I'll just give you a warning this time, but you need to slow down and drive safely. You have precious cargo." He glanced in my direction, probably impressed by my boots and Dale Evans skirt.

Mom's eyebrows shot up onto her forehead but, of course, the policeman didn't know her well enough to be intimidated. Her heart attack was a mild one, apparently, and the incident was never mentioned at home. There were too many other things for us to talk about. We had seen wild ponies and had met an actual literary celebrity!

We were like two friends.

Religion and Horses

Some of our neighbors spent their spare time at the American Legion. Others frequented the bowling alley and the local tavern. My family hung out at the little gray church on the corner, a block from our house. It wasn't my idea, but if you had to be religious, Presbyterian was the way to go.

My best friend, Laverne, was Catholic and had to go to confession on Saturdays when children were supposed to be having fun. I marveled that somebody so good could have anything to confess. I used to wonder if Laverne had to make up sins, but that would probably have been a sin itself. She never sassed her mother or chewed gum in school. If I'd been Catholic, I could have spent a whole day in confession.

Everybody felt sorry for the two Methodists in my sixth-grade class. They weren't allowed to play cards or go to the movies. My sister knew a girl in the ninth grade who couldn't dance, wear make-up, or wear shorts in hot weather because her church didn't approve. I'm not even kidding!

The best thing about Presbyterians was that we didn't get all excited in church, throwing our hands in the air and shouting "Amen!" or "Hallelujah," or calling out in "tongues." Our congregation just sat there quietly until it was time to sing a hymn, then the people who were still awake were allowed to stand up.

I gained even more appreciation for the Presbyterian church the summer our Baptist neighbor invited my sister to a revival meeting.

Her daughter was twelve years old like Janet. I tagged along because it was being held in a big round tent like the circus our parents had taken us to earlier that month, and I was curious. Big mistake.

This tent was crowded and stifling. It smelled worse than the circus and only had one ring. The ringmaster wore a black suit and carried a book. He looked like a magician, but Mrs. Smith said he was called an evangelist. He stood up after the choir finished singing.

He began calmly enough, this evangelist, sounding a lot like our preacher. But after a while, he took off his jacket, then his tie, and he rolled up his sleeves like he was going to change a tire. He shouted. He ranted. Saliva flew through the air as he waved the Bible and got up close to peoples' faces. He was kind of like a circus animal, and I was glad we were not seated on the aisle. Janet's eyes were as big and round as jelly donuts, so I tried to lighten the mood.

"We should have brought that roll of paper towels from the kitchen. We could probably sell them." But Janet shushed me and nodded toward our neighbor, whose expression reminded me of Dorothy's when she was clicking her heels and saying, "There's no place like home, there's no place like home."

For the better part of two hours, this evangelist dominated the steamy tent, preaching hellfire and damnation until his face was as red as the flames of hell, and he looked like he'd been standing under a lawn sprinkler. His shoes made squishy sounds when he walked by. All in all, he was scarier than any wild circus animal.

Toward the end, it was like a funeral. Men and women were

sobbing. Some streamed to the altar at the front of the tent and fell to the ground pleading to be saved. When a lady in the next row fainted, one of the ushers held something under her nose until she woke up. That's probably why it was called a revival.

I couldn't wait to tell my parents about this scary tent attraction that not only lacked clowns and cotton candy but was filled with creepy drama. Their reaction was even more shocking than the events of the evening.

"We had revivals down home," Mom told us, waving her hand to the side and making them sound as mundane as a church picnic. "I went once or twice to keep Mama company, but they're not for me."

"To each his own," Dad said, dunking a cookie in a cup of milk. "Some people put a lot of stock in revivals."

I thought my mother must have been mad to allow her innocent, impressionable daughters to attend such a gathering. But there was a method in her madness. After that night, I never again complained about going to church and sitting through boring sermons.

Well, hardly ever.

⚾ ⚾ ⚾ ⚾

There was something going on in our church every day of the week: Youth Group, Women of the Church, Men's Club, church dinners, Scouts, and so on. When the steeple bell chimed on Sunday mornings, it was more than a call to worship; it signaled the most important day of the week for the little gray-shingled church at the corner of Fullerton and Kenwood Avenues. My father was an elder and Sunday School superintendent. As his assistant and secretary, as well as president of the Women of the Church, Mom knew every-thing that was going on. It had been said more than once that Thelma Knobel had her finger in every pie.

Clearly, our family was religious, and when my mother told me that Jesus wanted me for a sunbeam, I believed her. People even joked that our dog had received a calling the Sunday morning he slipped through our front door and tracked our scent to church. He walked down the aisle during the sermon and flushed us out like a bevy of quail during hunting season—which was fine with me as I got to leave church early and take him back home. That said, my parents were not fanatics. They didn't approach innocent strangers and quote Scripture.

With freshly shampooed hair and polished shoes, we were among the first to arrive at church on Sunday morning and the last to leave Sunday afternoon. In good weather, we walked the block and a half from home. Most of the members knew me, which made slipping out of the sanctuary during sermons tricky. Through the years, Jesus's little sunbeam lost her shine from time to time. One Sunday I slipped through the side door on the pretext of using the two-seater, state-of the-art outhouse behind the church. With the sermon droning on and my allow-ance burning a hole in my pocket, I bolted across the street to Neutzel's Grocery Store. Minutes later, with all four sections of a Sky Bar crammed into my mouth and juice dripping on my chin, I climbed the wooden steps to the church porch in time to hear the benediction through the open door.

The adrenalin pumping through my body was almost as satis-fying as the delectable blending of my four favorite flavors as I merged into the stream of exiting worshipers.

"Is that chocolate on your face?" My mother asked when I joined her in the aisle. I swallowed the last sweet morsel and shook my head *no*, without a trace of guilt.

At the age of eight, I had no doubt that I was the most religious person in our family. I certainly spent more time in prayer than anybody else.

"Please, please God can I have a pony? There are so many in the world, and all I want is one. I promise to take care of him and do all my schoolwork and chores. Please, God!"

Who knew anyone was actually listening? Or that religion would be paying off for me in such a spectacular way—even if it did take so long?

⚾ ⚾ ⚾ ⚾

I was eleven the year religion finally paid off in the form of two strangers who appeared in our pew one Sunday morning—kind of like the angels who appeared to the shepherds in the Christmas story. After the service, my parents greeted the couple, as was their custom, and learned that they lived on a nearby farm.

And they had horses!

I was in the company of real horse people and stared until my eyes watered. The attractive, slender woman had dark hair pulled back into a neat bun like those women in foxhunting prints. Her name was Lois, and I pictured her in a derby, black jacket, britches, and high boots, mounted on a sleek chestnut hunter. He was Mr. Jackson, country squire, in a worn tweed jacket with a pipe and tobacco pouch protruding from the breast pocket. They were both brown and wrinkled from hours spent in the hunt field astride their warmblooded half-breds.

Without warning, Mom reached out and nudged me in their direction. A normal mother might have described me as horse-crazy. Not mine.

"This is our daughter, Peggy. She has been a devoted student of all things equine since she was born."

She sounded like a used car salesman and did everything but kick my tires. Normally, I'd have found her pretentious dribble and shameless promotion embarrassing, but I was mesmerized and fighting the urge to sniff their clothing.

Before leaving church, the couple invited me to visit their farm that very afternoon. They were angels for sure, leading the way to paradise. Mom seemed to understand when I was too excited to eat a bite of lunch.

All the horse books in the world could not have prepared me for the moment I slid onto that cow pony's round, furry back. I had spent the first eleven years of my life waiting for this moment and knew instinctively that having a living, breathing horse beneath me was a more spiritual experience than church could ever be.

Lois led the horse around the paddock the first time then turned the reins over to me and joined my mother at the fence. Chico's warmth radiated through me on that chilly April afternoon as I rode around and around the paddock bareback like a Comanche Indian. The books hadn't told me that, without a saddle, I would feel each and every movement of his powerful body.

"Are you sure she hasn't been around horses before?" I heard Lois say as I passed. "She is a natural! And so athletic!"

As I rode out of earshot, I hoped that my mother wasn't telling Lois about my backyard pony. That would be so embarrassing! As I've already mentioned, the thick grapevines that formed a border between our backyard and the alley were supported by a long, sturdy pole. For the past four years, that pole had served as my virtual pony. With an old sofa cushion for a saddle and clothesline for reins, I rode the prairie and rounded up strays.

Some mothers would have considered counseling. Mine, however, made saddlebags out of two old pocketbooks and, after my chores were completed, sent me off on cattle drives with a sandwich and grape juice, horse books, and a slicker for bad weather.

I rode my backyard pony in the heat of summer while my father cut the grass and my mother hung out the laundry, propping sagging lines high in the air with long wooden poles. I rode on autumn days when the wind howled through the canyons and tumbleweeds spooked my pony. I ignored the irony of a mount that shed in the fall instead of in the spring like other ponies and horses. In the dead of winter, when his coat had turned brown and fallen to the ground, he was little more than a skeleton of bare, twisted vines.

And then the angels appeared in Kenwood Presbyterian Church and sat in our pew.

I kept Chico at a walk that day, using the reins to turn him in big circles and change direction. As anxious as I was to jog and trot, I didn't want to fall off and break my neck in front of an audience.

I slid to the ground an hour later when Mom said, "We don't want to outstay our welcome, Peggy. I'm sure Lois has things to do."

As I hugged Chico around the neck, breathing in the heavenly horsey scent, the angel said to me, "I hope you'll come again, Peggy. I'm here every day."

I stored the memories away for later—the sound of Chico's hooves on the soft dirt, the jangle of the metal snaffle bit when he shook his head, the soft whinny to a stablemate, a magnificent bay Thoroughbred mare whose head hung over the barn door.

"Was it fun?" Dad asked at supper that night.

How could I tell him that I had felt at home on Chico's back? Or that it was where I was *meant* to be. That would sound silly. So I merely nodded and smiled.

"Lois couldn't believe that Peggy has never been around horses before," Mom said. "She is a natural! That's exactly what Lois said. She's a natural!" Then she looked my father right in the eye.

"I wonder if Peggy might be one of those child prodigies I've read about."

Dad just smiled and looked as happy as I felt, while Janet wondered if anyone else noticed a strange odor in the room. That night I gave the jeans that were covered in horsehair and sweat one last sniff before my mother took them off to the basement laundry room, but not before removing the handful of hay from the pocket for under my pillow.

Before long, I was spending afternoons and weekends in a little slice of horse heaven called Triangle Farm. Not only was I around horses, I was away from my mother, who couldn't tolerate idle hands. There was no such thing as lounging on the floor with Topper or leafing through the pages of a horse book while she was busy. The Disciple of Drudgery was always working, flitting here and there. Had she been a horse, she'd have been covered in lather.

Mrs. Jackson—Lois—looked forward to my visits and said she was grooming me to ride in horse shows. Ever cheerful, she would set down the brown bottle that was her constant companion and demonstrate horse care and riding technique. I brushed dried mud from Chico's coat, mucked the manure and urine-soaked straw from his stall, and rode bareback. Then I would hop on my bike and pedal the uphill-mile home where I stood on our tiny back porch and shed my offensive clothing while Mom shielded me from neighbors' eyes with a robe.

By summer, I had graduated to Maresy Doats, the beautiful family Thoroughbred, a dark bay mare with a star on her forehead. Sometimes on weekends, Lois's grown son, an accomplished rider, gave me lessons. A stickler for balance and form, he would lunge the mare on a long line while yelling, "Knees in! Heels down! Back straight!" while I rode with my arms folded across my chest. There was a God, no doubt about it!

"She used to be a racehorse," I told my parents. "Now Maresy's a hunter and pleasure horse with the most amazing gaits and perfect conformation!"

My mother couldn't wait to tell family and friends that her daughter was riding a Thoroughbred—with a saddle no less!

After we finished in the barn, Lois and I would retire to the house for a beer (well, a soda for me). She was never without a drink as we looked at photographs of horses, ribbons, and trophies. Sometimes she would put down her drink and play the piano. She was a more accomplished player than I was, but then, who wasn't? Typically, before I left for home, her speech would become slurred, and her eyelids heavy. One afternoon she even fell asleep in the paddock while sitting on Chico's back, a beer in one hand and reins in the other. Afraid she would fall off, I woke her up. I didn't mention it to my parents. There were no alcoholic beverages in our house; that would have set a poor example for my sister and me. I did, however, brag that my new friend was a talented musician.

Naturally, Mom told our preacher, who told the music director, who invited Lois to join the church choir. She had a deep voice and sang with the men. The choir loved her lighthearted spirit and sense of humor. "She keeps us laughing," quipped one of my mother's choir friends.

While I was combing manes and tails, Mom was combing secondhand shops for inexpensive riding clothes. She had a habit of showing up at the stable unexpectedly while I was soaping saddles or grooming horses. One day I heard her voice as I picked dirt from Maresy's hooves.

"You might have some nurturing instincts after all," she called from the fence.

"Gee, Mom, every time I look up, there you are checking on me like I was a kid!"

She took no notice.

Never mind. She would soon be up to her neck in preparations for my sister's sixteenth birthday bash to be held in our church basement hall. She'd forget all about me.

And still, she found time to stalk me.

That year my mentors took me to horse shows, club meetings, and even to taverns where I met an array of colorful, horsey characters— people who had nothing in common with my parents and their friends. Naturally, I kept that a secret. In contrast to his fun-loving wife, Mr. Jackson wore a perpetual frown. I had asked him once if he ever rode horseback.

"No," he said, "I just pay the bills." Lois's nickname for him was "Grumpy." They argued often and bitterly.

Before long, my mother was forced to face reality. Lois was up to the top of her riding boots in domestic turmoil and alcoholism. There were rumblings from choir members, as well.

"On rehearsal nights, the choir room reeks like a brewery! We have to open the windows!"

One Sunday morning, as the choir processed through the hallway on the way to the chancel, passing close to my mother and me, Lois paused. Polluting the air and slurring her words, she pronounced with exaggerated dignity, "I've memorized all fifteen verses of *The Shooting of Dan McGrew*, and I can't remember one word of this damn hymn." As Lois zigzagged down the aisle, my mother's eyebrows disappeared into her hairline. That was the last Sunday Lois sang in the Kenwood choir. I was, however, allowed to return to the farm to ride. For the time being, at least.

The final straw came on the day of the annual equestrian club show. I was meant to be an observer, but, at the last minute, I showed a little gray hunter for a friend of Lois. It was my first blue ribbon, and I couldn't wait to tell my parents.

On the way home, Lois instructed her husband to pull into the horsey set's favorite watering hole. He usually dozed in the car while she indulged at the bar with fellow equestrians. From time to time, Mr. Jackson strode in, grumbled, and stomped out.

I sipped Coca-Cola at a nearby table and listened to the crude banter. Later, as I basked in the odor of horses and beer, I heard the familiar slur of Lois's words. When she argued loudly with the bartender and slid off her stool onto the floor, I knew what I had to do. After helping her up, I found a telephone.

The stricken, angry faces of my parents appeared across the smoky tavern, and I feared that my little slice of horse heaven was going to evaporate like the foam on the mugs around me.

Unfortunately, I was right.

Family: For Better or Worse

I was pedaling my bike along the sidewalk on Leslie Avenue practicing my no-hands routine when a neighbor called to me.

"Hey, Peggy Knobel, are your parents running a boarding house? Every time I look, there's another stranger."

Before she finished her question, I was well on my way and gave her a shrug.

"A boarding house!?" my mother said. "Why can't people just mind their own business?"

When it came to neighbors, Mom was aloof. She was cordial enough when they met but would no more gossip over the backyard fence than wear curlers in her hair while hanging out the laundry. Hers was not a world of morning coffee klatches. She had followed her mother's counsel when moving to "the city."

"Thelma, don't get close to your neighbors," Grandma Daisy had said. "And whatever you do, don't let them know your business!"

In hindsight, the neighbor had a point. In the 1930s and '40s, my mother was the Harriet Tubman of our family, running her own version of the Underground Railroad. One by one as her siblings finished high school, she brought them from the small fishing village in Fleeton, Virginia, to our home in Baltimore, where they lived until they found work, job training, or a husband.

Dad had grown up in an austere home and welcomed Mom's cheerful family with open arms. What had begun as a "Depression migration" became a coming-of-age rite of passage for Mom's sisters.

With just three bedrooms, our house wasn't large, but every inch was lived in. There were no rooms that were off limits or furniture you weren't allowed to use, unlike my friend's house where sofa cushions were wrapped in plastic and lampshades, in cellophane.

For our country aunts, the two-story, brown-shingled house on Leslie Avenue was the equivalent of a five-star hotel, with such luxurious amenities as indoor plumbing, central heating, electricity, and a state-of-the-art black telephone.

When it came to her siblings, Mom was like a proud parent, seeing signs of greatness in each of them.

Aunt Betty (Orvetta) was the Florence Nightingale of the Williams family. Before joining the Army, she went to nursing school and then lived with us while working at Johns Hopkins Hospital. The go-to person for all our health-related concerns, her medical expertise was held in high regard in our house. She was a great proponent of castor oil . . . but I loved her anyway. Later, when Aunt Betty began painting, her waterscapes graced our walls. Through the years, the amateurish pieces were relegated to the bedrooms, while her more sophisticated artwork gave our living room a touch of class. They allowed Mom to brag about her sister without actually speaking.

Aunt Elvira was sweet and creative, or, as Mom liked to say, "fixy." When Elvira lived with us, there was lace on our bathroom towels, tassels on the sofa pillows, and cheerful flower arrangements on the dining room table—but not the kind one sees in church or the funeral parlor. She was, without question, the Martha Stewart of her time. Once, when I was being *unfairly* punished, she slipped me a handful of pennies while my mother wasn't looking. Aunt Elvira was the least worldly and sophisticated of the sisters, and my parents felt protective towards her. Even after she married a Baltimore man and settled nearby, we remained close.

Aunt Nealie (Cornelia) was beautiful and stylish and traveled with a suitcase filled with toiletries and makeup. She was forever combing our hair and fussing over Janet and me (when she could catch me). She married a man she met while living with us and, after moving to Nebraska, sent us delightful packages in the mail. My favorite was a fringed buckskin jacket that caused friction between my mother and me.

It was just like the one Annie Oakley wore in pictures. Poor Janet received a fancy case full of makeup. I felt sorry for her, but she took it well. *Pretending* to be excited, she ran up the stairs to her bedroom so that we wouldn't see her disappointment.

"Please, Mom, can I wear my jacket to church with my cowboy boots?" I begged. "Please?!"

"Peggy, your father is a church leader. I don't think he'd appreciate his daughter showing up in a fringed cowboy jacket."

Even at my tender age, I knew a bogus argument when I heard it. Dad knew only one thing about fashion—if it was on the bedside chair, he could wear it. My father might have been perceived as head of our family, but that was only because Mom wanted it that way. She liked to give the appearance of being in his shadow, but I knew who made the rules.

Mom and I came to a compromise. What a sight we Knobels must have been walking down the aisle on that early-August morning (long before air conditioning came to Kenwood Church). Dad in his Sunday best, my stylishly dressed mother, and the lovely Janet, straight from the pages of *Seventeen* magazine, wearing for the first time a hint of coral lipstick and a faint blush.

Bringing up the rear was Annie Oakley. The long fringe on her jacket swaying to and fro as she lumbered down the aisle in her black patent leather shoes, her six-shooter checked at the door.

Uncle Charles visited our home, too, but he wasn't looking for work; he had his eye on the pretty girl across the street. There was never any doubt that he would follow in his daddy's footsteps as a waterman when he left the Navy. It was obvious that he held a special place in Mom's heart. Once when he carried me on his shoulders, I hit my head on a ceiling beam. He laughed at me when I cried and didn't even get hollered at. He married the pretty girl across the street, became a fish boat captain like my grandfather, and kept us supplied with fish, soft crabs, and oysters through the years—my mother's favorite foods in the whole world.

Vivacious Aunt Mary, the baby of the Williams family, went to secretarial school and filled our house with laughter and excitement.

"She's too popular for her own good," Mom used to say.

"Honestly, Thelma, it's a wonder I have any dates at all, after you give them the third degree," Aunt Mary complained, rolling her eyes. But Mom didn't care. She wasn't about to shirk her responsibilities, staying awake nights until her little sister came through the front door, no matter how late.

Our home remained the family gathering place through the years. The five sisters were like the characters from *Little Women*, with their stories of sewing bees, taffy pulls around the dining room table, and clambakes on the beach.

"When we were teenagers, your mother used our parties to get the housecleaning done," Aunt Elvira reminisced. This didn't surprise me at all.

Aunt Nealie would invariably chime in, mimicking my mother in a theatrical way that Janet and I would never have dared.

"Well, sure, we can have a party, but first we need to clean. We wouldn't want our friends to see the house looking like this, now would we?"

Aunt Betty would look at Janet and me and add, "Then your mother would say, 'And while we're at it, we'll just make new curtains and hang wallpaper.'"

Mom laughed good-naturedly at the stories, explaining to Janet and me, "Your grandmother wasn't interested in decorating."

I admired Grandma all the more, if that was possible. The heart and soul of the Williams family, she was my hero—a fearless, ax-wielding woman in an apron, chasing squawking roosters across the yard. Grandma Daisy might not have been in tune to the finer aspects of decorating, but she had the best garden in Fleeton and could wring the necks of chickens in record time while singing "In the Garden" without missing a beat.

Of course, people never heard about that side of Grandma from my mother. She chose to accentuate Grandma's gentler side. She once told a group of church ladies:

"My mother was a gentle woman who walked us children across the road to St. Mary's Episcopal Church Sunday mornings, then spent the afternoon playing hymns on the upright piano in the parlor. She was a woman of quiet strength and moral conviction. I can still see her worn black Bible on the kitchen windowsill."

We visited Grandma often, our favorite place away from home. Fleeton was small, as in one road that made a loop at the end of the peninsula. It was a place where grizzled men in overalls left home to work on fish boats. Often gone for days at a time, their women tended the houses and gardens and raised the children in their absence.

Rounding the last bend in that road to Grandma Daisy's was like stepping through the magic wardrobe into Narnia, except for the mythical beasts.

The closest thing to talking animals in Fleeton were Grandma's chickens who literally squawked their heads off when she picked up her ax.

Fleeton was wonderfully behind the times when it came to indoor plumbing and electricity. At home we never got to brush our teeth in the backyard in our pajamas and spit on the grass. Or bathe with a basin of water, or wee in a bucket at night. The same mother who acted ashamed of me when I was a horse galloping through the neighborhood at home laughed out loud when I ran through the marsh grasses with the salty wind on my face. Fleeton was a vacation from strict routine and my mother's close scrutiny.

⚾ ⚾ ⚾ ⚾

Growing up with relatives who loved me as much as my parents did had not prepared me for Cousin Jimmy. Nothing could have. I was twelve the year my mother's nephew came to live with us.

It was evident from the beginning that Cousin Jimmy was no ordinary relative. It wasn't just the way Mom was tearing through my old bedroom like the cyclone from *The Wizard of Oz*, scrubbing walls, beating rugs, and washing curtains. I had seen her prepare for visiting relatives my entire life. When she reached into the cedar chest and retrieved her treasured heirloom bedspread, I knew Cousin Jimmy was special indeed. I hadn't seen those colorful embroidered flowers since the night we hosted our church's visiting minister and his wife. When she placed a vase of freshly cut lilacs on the old chest of drawers, I said, "Boy, you'd think Cousin Jimmy was the Second Coming!"

"No, this is his *first* visit."

Biblical humor was wasted on my mother. When it came to religion, she was deadly serious.

"What's he like?" I had never met Cousin Jimmy. He was a grandson from Grandpop's first wife and had grown up in another town. Mom's next statement said it all.

"Your cousin is the first college graduate in our family! And he's going to be a schoolteacher!" She made it sound like he was the president. I knew it was going to be a long year.

Then she muttered something under her breath. "He's probably still a little peculiar."

Now this got my attention because ours was a house of rules, and Mom had just broken the most important one: *Thou shalt not criticize a relative.* Or, as she was fond of saying, "If you can't say something nice, don't say anything at all!"

There were other rules. They might not have been chiseled in stone, but they were right up there with the Ten Commandments, and I knew them by heart. *Thou shalt not skip church or Sunday School*, for instance. There were exceptions, of course. If you were dead—or completely paralyzed. I got a special dispensation when I had scarlet fever and there was a quarantine sign on the door.

One of Mom's rules was directed straight at me. *Thou shalt pay attention in class and do thy homework.*

Even Topper had one: *Thou shalt stay off the furniture!*

Sometimes rules collided, like these two: *Guests in our home will be treated with respect at all times* and, *Thou shalt not use crude language.* When this happened, my mother would have to choose which rule to honor. Once when Aunt Mary and my cousins were visiting from the country, we played 500 Rummy around the enamel-top kitchen table with Topper at our feet. During the game, my cousin suddenly sprang from the chair and waved her hands in front of her face.

"Peggy, your dog just farted!"

Now *fart* was considered a crude term. It could sound like a fart and smell like a fart, but in our house, it was *gas*. Topper didn't fart. He passed gas. Aunt Mary was twelve when I was born and had been calling me *Fart-Blossom* for as long as I could remember (when her big sister wasn't around). For a while, I thought Fart-Blossom was my name.

Instead of admonishing a guest in our home for using crude language, Mom merely raised her eyebrows and ushered Topper out the back door.

⚾ ⚾ ⚾ ⚾

"What do you mean, *he's peculiar?*" I asked my mother.

"Cousin Jimmy's just a little different, that's all," she said, leveling her gaze at me. "But he's a good boy and will be treated with respect while he's in our home! *Won't he?*" It was more a threat than a question.

I'm not sure what I expected of the recent college graduate and soon-to-be schoolteacher, but it wasn't the skinny, sickly looking specimen we picked up from the bus terminal that summer afternoon.

"I have a low resistance and weak sinuses," our cousin explained as he unpacked a vaporizer and bottles of tonic and vitamins.

Jimmy's skin had a grayish pallor, similar to what the dog threw up after foraging through the neighbors' garbage. And he was the fidgety type, with his feet in constant motion even when he was sitting.

Worst of all were the frightful sounds he made as he cleared his throat and sinuses—noises that would have gotten me sent from the room. Even my mother was not prepared for such drama that first evening Cousin Jimmy joined us for dinner. We had made it through Dad's prayer and were well into our meatloaf and mashed potatoes when Cousin Jimmy laid his hand to the side of his nose, tilted his head, and honked like a barnyard goose during mating season.

Mom, who was self-control personified, had a low startle threshold. She dropped her fork and grabbed onto the table as though we were having a magnitude 7 earthquake. When I erupted in convulsive laughter, more from shock than anything, she shot me a warning frown, as if I had any control at all. My sister exhibited amazing control. But I knew what was happening behind the napkin covering the lower half of my father's face.

Just as I was getting a grip on myself, another mighty honk erupted, and the entire table vibrated. I knew I would be on thin ice, but I couldn't help myself.

"Jimmy," I said, "you snort like Mr. Sippel's hogs at feeding time." Sure enough, my mother's eyebrows shot up like a rocket. Even more shocking than those barnyard sounds was the fact that Cousin Jimmy seemed entirely unaware. His face was without expression, as innocent as Topper's when he was farting after feasting on the neighbor's garbage.

I tried not to laugh; I really did. But everything seems funnier when you know you *shouldn't* laugh. On more than one occasion, I was excused until I could get control of myself.

Of course, my mother was ready to accept anything from this college graduate and soon-to-be schoolteacher and, truth be told, we gradually became desensitized to his eccentricities.

There was nothing I liked about our peculiar visitor. He was an unwelcome intrusion in our home. But in fairness to Cousin Jimmy, I was twelve that year and mad at the world. A living, breathing horse had been yanked from under me, and I missed the furry coat and muzzle nuzzling against my neck. I missed the

My parents, Carl and
Thelma, "Young love"

Our family: Thelma,
Carl, Janet, and Peg

Back: My sister Janet, and a friend
Front: Peggy and my
best friend, Laverne

My mom, Thelma, 1940

Thelma and Carl

Thelma and Carl 1955

Carl and Thelma out on the town

Peggy after school, 1948
"Rotten to the core."

Peggy, 1948

Peggy and Janet, Christmas 1941

My mother's first surprise Christmas gift: a
portrait of Janet and Peggy, 1950

The "old" Kenwood Church, built in 1927,
was our second home, 1948

Peggy in a second-hand riding outfit, 1950

The current Kenwood Presbyterian Church was built
in 1950, on the same property as the old church.

The Williams Family.
Top: Aunt Elvira, Uncle Charles,
Aunt Mary, and Thelma
Bottom: Grandma Daisy,
Aunt Betty, and Grandpop
(Captain Charlie)

Carl riding a bike on
Leslie Avenue

Uncle Charles and Grandma Daisy

[Back row, left to right and then front row, left to right]
Aunt Mary, Uncle Charles, Aunt Cornelia, Aunt Elvira,
Aunt Betty, Grandma Daisy, and Thelma

The Williams sisters later in life: Aunt Mary, Aunt
Cornelia, Aunt Elvira, Aunt Betty, and Thelma

The Great Wicomico River Light by Aunt Betty (Orvetta Harvey)

Jet

Peggy on Jet

"Paradise"

Farmhouse and bank barn on Trumps Mill Road

Thelma and Shaker

Thelma on Shaker

Peggy in a homemade
"ratcatcher" shirt with Topper

Coed Peggy and Missy, 1956

Carl and Thelma

Thelma

Thelma and Peggy, 1960

Peggy and John

John, 1953

Peggy, 1960

John and Peggy (wearing
a homemade coat with a
Hutzler's label), 1969

Scott, Phil, and Mike, 1969

John and Phil driving Tammy, 1971

Mike, Peggy, Scott, and Phil

sweet smell of clover hay in the barn and the odor of my jeans after riding bareback.

Ordinarily, I took out my resentment on our neighbors, sneaking outside after dark and throwing stones onto their roofs or ringing their doorbells and running off. I even overturned the occasional garbage can and threw rotting tomatoes at passing cars. Finding reasons to hate Cousin Jimmy was like shooting fish in a barrel.

There were two things in my cousin's favor: my mother was now preoccupied with gourmet meals and extra laundry (which gave me more freedom to run amuck), and we now had dessert every night.

Evenings, I looked forward to locking myself in the bathroom with one of Dad's Lucky Strike cigarettes. Sitting on the toilet seat blowing smoke through an open window (and coughing) couldn't compare to sitting on a Thoroughbred, but I found it weirdly gratifying—that is, until the college graduate began monopolizing our only bathroom with long, therapeutic, steamy baths.

"Steam opens the sinuses," he'd say afterwards, vanishing down the hall in a towel, chased by a cloud, while I danced a jig outside the bathroom door with a cigarette in my pocket.

Before long, the bathroom wallpaper peeled off like dead skin after a bad sunburn.

No matter what I said or did, I couldn't turn my mother against him.

"Look, Mom, Jimmy's steam made the bathroom wallpaper fall off," I'd say.

"Oh, I've been planning to brighten those walls with a coat of yellow paint, anyway," she said.

When our record player disappeared from the music room and Liszt's Hungarian Rhapsodies blared from my old upstairs bedroom, Janet and I both complained.

"Jimmy is bringing us culture," Mom said.

Dinnertime had all the ambiance of a group therapy session with Dr. Freud weighing in on my shortcomings.

"Peggy's going through that awkward stage." Or, "Peggy needs to work on a more refined smile." He even went so far as to say, "One day, Peggy might develop some grace and poise like her sister."

My mother hung on his every word as though he were some Old Testament prophet.

One evening after Dad had finished grace and Jimmy was cutting his roast beef, our star boarder asked if he might have a glass of wine. "Not only does red wine complement meat—it's a proven fact that it aids in digestion."

I looked at my mother in great anticipation, knowing that Cousin Jimmy stood a better chance of being served an appetizer of fried tarantula than he did of getting a glass of wine in our house. The mere presence of alcohol in the pantry would be a corrupting influence on two innocent children.

"I'm sorry, Jimmy," Mom said. "We don't keep alcohol in the house."

"Why don't you just turn your water into wine?" I was using the flippant tone I had adopted when addressing him. Again, no credit for a biblical reference, although there was a hint of a smile on Dad's lips.

Then Jimmy said something shocking.

"I saw you riding your bicycle, Peggy. I've never ridden a bike. Is it fun?"

This confirmed what I had suspected all along: my cousin had been raised in a jungle by chimpanzees. Naturally, I didn't voice my thoughts; I didn't have a death wish. Instead, I said, "But . . . *everybody* knows how to ride a bike."

"Carl and Peggy would love to teach you," my mother said, while I gagged on my beef.

For the next two afternoons, Dad and I ran alongside my wobbling bike like we were Secret Service agents protecting the president. Just when it looked like he might be getting the hang of it, he ran straight into the gutter that ran in front of our house and flipped over the handlebars.

"Riding a bicycle is too dangerous for an adult," he said, picking himself up. And that was that. So, with a touch of cruelty, I told him that my father loved nothing better than taking a spin along Leslie Avenue on my bicycle in the evening.

I envied Janet. "Just ignore him," she'd tell me. "Be polite, and pretend he isn't even here." That was easy for her to say. She'd soon be leaving for college, and I'd be stuck sitting across the dinner table from a honking hypochondriac.

Halfway through the summer, Jimmy was hired by the Board of Education. If I thought he had enjoyed a privileged status in our house before, his position now could only be described as exalted. While I was picturing my cousin entertaining a class of junior high-school students with his barnyard impersonations, my mother was holding him up to me as a model of success.

"See what an education can accomplish?" And then, just as boys graduated from knickers into grown-up long pants, Cousin Jimmy graduated to a grown-up name.

"It's time we started calling him, Jim," Mom decided. "It's more befitting than Jimmy for someone of his position."

My father took Jim car shopping and gave him driving lessons. Thanks to his patience, Dad was everybody's driving instructor of choice. Jim's 1950 chartreuse convertible with leopard skin seat covers stood out in our dull, middle-class neighborhood like a belly dancer at an Amish funeral.

The day he finally got his license—after the third try—Jim put the top down and corralled our family for a victory lap. Janet and I sank low in the backseat alongside Mom, and Dad tried to look calm as Jim barreled toward stop signs laughing like a hyena.

It was at one such stop that I would feel a rare, close bond with my sister. Janet was always sweet and kind to me, but we shared little besides a bedroom. She was popular and active in normal teenage pursuits while I ran the streets impersonating a juvenile delinquent. As my mother held onto the strap by the window, my ladylike sister put her lips to my ear and whispered, "He thinks he's hot shit!"

I jerked my head around and gave her a wicked grin. If she was looking for an accomplice to help her kill him in his sleep, she needed to look no further.

Mom's comment was more diplomatic when we returned to the curb with thumping hearts and Phyllis Diller hairdos.

"Well, you don't lack confidence, Jim. I'll give you that."

I looked at Janet hopefully in case there were other insights she wished to share, but that was the extent of her disdain.

⚾ ⚾ ⚾ ⚾

At about this time, I had two close calls that put an end to my crime spree. One evening when Dad was at Lions Club, my mother sent me around to Baker's Store for a loaf of bread. On the way, I rang some doorbells, jumped over the railings, and scampered off like a common criminal. Coming home, I gathered handfuls of pebbles and threw them onto our neighbors' roofs, then lurked in the shadows as porch lights flickered on. When I opened our kitchen door, my mother was on the telephone.

"No, Mrs. Smith, we haven't had any problems with the neighborhood children. Well, I'm sure you're mistaken. Peggy wouldn't do anything like that, but I'll ask her if she knows who did."

Without looking at me, she took the bread, the receipt, and her change.

"Mrs. Smith says somebody has been throwing stones at her house again. She thought it might be you."

I shook my head no and frowned at the very thought.

"I told her she was mistaken." And then my mother looked deep into my eyes. "Because it would hurt your father to hear that you had done something like that. And I know you wouldn't want to hurt your father."

Saying nothing, I ran up the stairs where I fell onto my bed crying. Everything was wrong. I longed for Chico and Maresy Doats, to brush their coats and feel the warmth of their breath on my cheek and to canter around the field. And now, the thought of hurting my father was too much to bear. As usual, my mother had seen right through me and forced me to take a look at myself. What I saw wasn't pretty. When I remembered the trash can I had overturned in the street minutes earlier, I felt a new shame.

One thing I was sure of: I had thrown my last stone, rung my last doorbell, and dumped my last trash can. I had already thrown my last tomato at a car the night I hit my target, and a man slammed on his breaks and chased me down the dark alley. He was quick as lightning, but I knew the neighborhood like the back of my hand and lost him when I skirted a barbecue pit and jumped a fence on Linhigh Avenue. Still, I had lain awake all night with my eyes wide open.

⚾ ⚾ ⚾ ⚾

In the days that followed, I took Janet's advice and tried to ignore Jim's flamboyance behind the wheel dressed in a ridiculous black turtleneck and jaunty beret. I even forgave him for invading my territory, stealing our record player, and monopolizing the bathroom. But when he stole my most treasured possession, it was impossible to look the other way.

Topper and I were the Lassie and Timmy of Leslie Avenue. When he wasn't racing beside my bike or hiding behind bushes with me during nightly games of Redline, he was stretched out on the floor at my side while I struggled with arithmetic.

Jim had coveted my sleek whippet from the day he arrived, calling him a noble beast and saying, "Topper has the demeanor of a royal palace dog."

"Hey," I said running down the stairs one afternoon. "Jimmy just put my dog in his car and drove off with him! He can't do that!"

My mother wasn't worried. "Jim thinks a lot of Topper. He'll take care of him."

I didn't blame Topper. As far as he was concerned, riding in a car beside an open window was right up there with raiding neighbors' garbage cans after dark and slinking onto soft, upholstered furniture when my mother wasn't around.

Before long, Jim began enticing Topper to his room and subjecting him to the likes of Bizet or Olivier's *Hamlet*.

"He's holding my dog captive!" I grumbled. "Topper's probably on his bed right now eating cookies!"

"Don't be silly," my mother said. "Jim knows the rules." What she meant, of course, was, "Jim is a responsible schoolteacher; he doesn't break rules."

That very evening while my parents were figuring estimates and typing bills at the dining room table, I was struggling with square roots alone on the floor and thinking how unfair life was. Suddenly, a blood-curdling shriek sent us flying up the stairs to my old room.

My parents stood gasping in the doorway. "What in the world?" my mother asked.

"Is everything okay?" asked Dad, fanning the air. I arrived in time to see Topper leaping from the bed, having heaved the contents of the Smith's garbage can onto Mom's cherished heirloom spread—not that you could appreciate the colorful embroidered flowers at that point. Blaring from my record player in the corner were the dramatic strains of Ravel's "Bolero." As my parents forced open the windows, Jim pushed me aside, gagged, and flew down the hall.

I tried not to gloat when I joined my mother at the kitchen table for a cup of hot cocoa before bed. Seeing the uppity schoolteacher get his comeuppance was going to be delicious.

"I don't believe I ever told you about Jim's father," Mom began as she stirred her drink. She looked tired from the massive cleanup, as Jimmy had not quite made it into the bathroom before losing his supper. Her expression was sad, and I was afraid she was going to tell me something that would make me sympathetic toward the peculiar relative who had made my life miserable.

I heard a story about an abusive, alcoholic husband and father. A father who had beat his sickly son for falling into a well. When the father died young, the son was raised by his overprotective mother and spinster aunt. It must have pained my mother to speak of relatives in such a way.

I would understand later that this was an explanation for the tolerance my mother had shown a nephew who was *a little peculiar*.

I was twelve the year I learned tolerance for a fellow misfit, a relative who was still finding his way. It was the year my mother learned that teachers are human. Of course, *I* already knew that.

Mom had been right about Jim bringing us culture. He introduced me to my favorite new song, Ravel's "Bolero."

Paradise Found

Sashaying around the neighborhood in a provocative fishnet blouse like a prostitute on the prowl was out of character for me. Yet it's exactly what I did. Who could believe that such promiscuous behavior would have such astonishing results?

At thirteen, Laverne and I weren't as close as we'd been as kids, but we had maintained a friendly relationship of sorts—despite the fact that I had convinced her that piano lessons were great fun (kind of like Tom Sawyer had persuaded his friends that whitewashing a fence was fun). She didn't hold it against me since her mother wasn't as steeped in culture as mine and allowed her to stop the lessons when she'd had enough. By the same token, I didn't resent Laverne because my mother had always held her up as a model, saying things like, "Peggy, you could look as pretty as Laverne if you used your hair brush." I heard this as she was wrestling my hair into braids, comparing my hair to Brer Rabbit's briar patch.

Polite and ladylike, Laverne was still the gold standard as far as Mom was concerned. A month earlier, she had practically forced me to accompany my old friend to the new community teen center. For two hours, I stood awkwardly on the sidelines like a scarecrow in a cornfield while Laverne made easy conversation with boys. I watched her dance to the music of Patti Page and Nat King Cole, her curly blonde ponytail swaying back and forth like the metronome on Mrs. Schiffler's piano. It was my first and last visit to the teen center.

"Hey, Peggy, let's take a walk to the five-and-dime," Laverne called to me from her front porch one day. *You-know-who* was thrilled and gave me an advance on my allowance. At Woolworth, we were mesmerized by a window display of flashy, seductive shirts. Perhaps it was the colorful elasticized tube top that caught my attention or maybe it was the overlay of what looked like the netting my Uncle Charles used for catching menhaden fish. It was my first experience clothes shopping, and I felt quite grown up as I plunked down my allowance beside Laverne's.

I was pretty sure my sophisticated sister wouldn't be caught dead wearing a sexy fishnet blouse, but she had just left for college in Virginia, so I wouldn't have to answer to her. At thirteen, I had become an only child with a big bedroom all to myself, twice as many chores as ever, and no closer to having a horse.

"Let's take a walk around the block after dinner," Laverne suggested. "We can show off our new tops."

Accessorized with my best shorts and my mother's bright red lipstick, my fetching fishnet blouse and I slipped out the basement door unnoticed. For the next hour, my friend and I strolled the streets hoping to be noticed. I wondered if Laverne was gathering material for the confessional.

Except for the color, our new blouses were identical, yet I couldn't help but notice how the tube top on Laverne's blouse rested comfortably against the natural curves of her body. Being challenged in the natural curves department myself, my tube top plunged to my waist like baggy socks fell around my ankles. I reached under the netting and pulled it up repeatedly, finally resorting to holding it in place. I knew for certain that the car horns and wolf whistles were not directed at me.

My parents were working at the dining room table when I sneaked through the front door and up the stairs. Mom had her back to me, but the expression on my father's face was one I hadn't seen since the evening Topper left the steaming puddle on my mother's embroidered bedspread.

"What in the world was that get-up?" I heard him ask, which was odd, because Dad didn't notice things like clothes. A couple of days later he did something odd. He invited me to accompany him on his rounds.

Going on jobs with Dad was a rare treat since Mom didn't approve.

"It's no environment for a young lady! The men can be crude," she'd say.

A day away from "the slave driver" was a day without Tchaikovsky and housework. After checking on a couple of jobs, Dad and I came upon a field with horses.

"Look!" I shouted. But Dad had already pulled to the curb and shut off the engine.

"This is Bill's place," he said, lighting a cigarette and holding it out the window.

"You didn't tell me you knew somebody with horses—and so close to home!"

"I knew Bill when we were boys. At one time, his family owned all of this land around here. Hundreds of acres," he said, gesturing to the neighborhood of new, cookie-cutter duplex houses.

Two horses were leaning across a wire fence, straining to nibble tufts of pale green grass by the curb. The gray gelding had long shaggy fetlocks and abundant manure stains on his rump and shoulders. He had rubbed the top of his tail against a tree trunk or other object until the stubbly hairs looked like a porcupine's.

The other horse was a lovely reddish bay mare with a thick, unruly black mane. Her dusty coat said that she had just rolled in the dirt.

They weren't classy Thoroughbreds like Maresy Doats, but they were beautiful all the same. At the edge of the pasture, stood a ramshackle stable constructed from scraps of wood and corrugated metal. At first glance, it reminded me of Grandma's quilts. One of the pieces of siding was a weathered wooden yellow sign with the word "DETOUR" printed upside down in faded black letters. The patchwork building was dwarfed by the mountain of manure piled alongside.

"Bill lives with his mother and has never worked a day in his life, as far as I know. He's eccentric." My father spoke in a matter-of-fact, nonjudgmental tone.

"He devotes his life to animals."

In all, there were six horses. One of them drank from a dented metal trash can by the fence. The green hose coming from the can trailed up the hill to a small white bungalow.

When a blue convertible with bales of hay jutting from the gaping trunk roared into the driveway, the horses lifted their heads and trotted to the stable whinnying. Dad checked his watch.

A man with orangey-red hair emerged from the car wearing riding britches and boots while a menagerie of dogs and cats appeared from nowhere, panting and barking and rubbing against his legs. The door to the little white house opened, and a black and white sheepdog with three legs hobbled down the hill, his tail wagging.

I looked at Dad, who flicked away his cigarette, grinned, and pulled into the driveway behind the convertible.

I liked Bill from the beginning. He was the real thing.

"I volunteer with the Humane Society," he said, reaching down and picking up a scruffy black cat named Judy. "All of these animals were abused or neglected before they were rescued."

He took dog biscuits from his pocket as horses whinnied by the stable door. Bill shared his philosophy in three simple statements.

"Most people can't be trusted to care for animals. No matter how good their intentions, they'll let the animal down in the end. I've never sold an animal in my life, and I never will!"

He had a friendly smile, and I admired his fierce sense of devotion.

"Your father tells me you like horses."

⚾ ⚾ ⚾ ⚾

"Does Mom know Bill?" I asked on the way home, knowing that future visits depended on her approval. "Has she seen his—uh—farm?"

"Not yet, but she will."

As sure as the sun comes up, my mother would be vetting Bill and his farm, just as she had stood at the fence and watched the proceedings at Triangle Farm.

With optimism, I reminded myself that she had accepted a peculiar nephew. Maybe she would accept an eccentric horseman.

As I'd expected, my mother insisted on driving me for my next visit. The expression on her face as we drove up to the dilapidated stable said that we had stumbled upon some Third World slum.

I introduced her to Bill and then to the horses, especially Jet— the shaggy, half-broken, three-year-old gray gelding I had fallen head over heels in love with on my first brief visit.

Mom took one look at his ragged mane and tail, long shaggy fetlocks, and abundant manure stains, and lifted her eyebrows.

"He looks wild!"

"He's young and hasn't been handled much," I said.

"Hmmm . . . he'd be at home in front of a plow."

"He's part Percheron. That's a draft breed. His coat will turn lighter as he matures." I had read about the breed after my first visit.

My mother, who had been polite to Bill's face, seemed distracted on the drive home.

"Bill reminds me of Dr. Doolittle. Remember those stories you used to read to me?" She nodded but didn't respond.

In desperation, I said, "Did you notice that Bill smells like horses and not beer?" But she was far away, beyond my reach.

Despite my mother's reservations, I was allowed to return to the farm, where I helped with the grooming and stable work. We sometimes rode the trails together, Bill on his favorite bay mare, Cindy, and me on the young Jet.

If Mom had concerns about Bill, she didn't voice them to me, except to say that he was exploiting my labor. I assured her I loved every minute of it. My father visited often when he dropped me off or picked me up. He'd chat a few minutes with Bill and then be on his way. One Saturday morning Dad wired Bill's stable for electricity—two simple light bulbs that Bill said would change his life.

As bad luck would have it, Bill's farm was near enough to the Elmwood Music Studio for me to ride my bike to my Tuesday piano lessons. After I had mucked stalls and groomed horses, my long-suffering piano teacher could smell me coming. To her credit, she resisted the urge to draw the curtains and lock the door. Instead, she smiled good-naturedly while I removed my boots then nodded toward the stairs where a bar of Lifebuoy soap awaited on the bathroom sink.

At the end of summer, the gods smiled, and Mrs. Schiffler called my mother.

"I'm afraid Peggy's heart isn't in this, Mrs. Knobel. That might change some day, but for now, I feel guilty accepting your money."

Praise the Lord! A little horse sweat and manure had accomplished what I'd failed to do in five years.

The fishnet blouse mysteriously disappeared from my bottom dresser drawer; I wasn't sure when. Unlike the *Titanic*, her maiden voyage had accomplished miraculous things. I remember her fondly.

⚾ ⚾ ⚾ ⚾

The sight of my mother and father sitting in our living room on a weekday afternoon was unnerving. I was reminded of the death of my grandfather when relatives sat unnaturally still beside the coffin in my aunt's parlor.

I might have worried that some other beloved family member had died but for my parents' cheerful expressions. I shuddered to think that they might have been engaging in a little afternoon intimacy. I had heard of such goings on from the more mature kids at school, but surely not in broad daylight.

I couldn't be in trouble. I'd walked the straight and narrow since discovering Bill's place. There was no way I was going to jeopardize my visits to the big gray horse I'd fallen in love with. These days, I tackled chores with the cheerfulness of Rebecca of Sunnybrook Farm and completed school assignments with the efficiency of my sister. My reign of terror in the neighborhood had come to an end without disgrace, and, at the age of fourteen, I was a model citizen and dutiful daughter.

Yet, there they were sitting on the living room sofa at 3:30 in the afternoon. Normally, I returned from school to the aroma of chicken soup or beef stew or apple pie. Today it was the scent of Dad's Old Spice aftershave. He wore a pale blue shirt the shade of his eyes and a pair of khakis with a crease as sharp as the ax that rested against Grandma Daisy's chopping block. Mom was her usual presentable self.

"What's up?"

"Your father and I are going to take you for a little ride."

It sounded so creepy I had to chuckle. My friend's father regularly threatened to take their disobedient dog for a little ride. A little *one-way* ride.

"Can't it wait? Bill's away, and I have to feed the horses."

"It won't take long," said my father. "We'll drop you at the stable afterwards."

"And wait for you," my mother added with a sniff that said, *No argument!* She still hovered, the way she had at the Jacksons' farm, popping up at the most inopportune times, like a television commercial interrupting *The Lone Ranger*.

The fact that I was happy helped Mom overlook the shabby appearance of Bill's farm, or as she described it, "the neighborhood eyesore."

Still, I lived in fear that one day she would throw up her hands and say, "Enough! No daughter of mine is going to spend her time in this junkyard!"

There was one event that especially worried me. One day when Bill was away, some older, teenaged would-be cowboys were hanging around the stable showing off and using foul language. They wanted to rent some horses and gallop over the countryside like a posse. I told them it wasn't a livery stable and continued cleaning stalls.

What I didn't realize was that my mother had chosen this time to drop by and was at that very moment standing just outside the door. After getting an eyeful, as well as an earful, she came bursting in like a whirlwind.

"You boys cannot be here when Mr. Bill isn't home." Startled, the three teenagers looked up. "Who says?"

My mother folded her arms, stood her ground, and did what she did best.

"Leave. Now!" she said, her eyebrows out of sight.

I held my breath, gripping the pitchfork tightly and hoping I wouldn't have to come to her defense.

The boys looked at my mother's no-nonsense expression for only seconds before slumping away.

I didn't know what to feel that day as we put my bike into the trunk of our car and headed home. I was angry, for sure, at being hauled off like a kid yet strangely in awe of my mother's triumphant standoff at the OK Corral. Was she afraid of *anything*? I could still see her face as she confronted those boys. It wasn't the first time I'd witnessed that expression. I had seen it the day she and Dad rescued me from a saloon where my drunken friend, Lois, had fallen off her barstool. Most of all, I had been afraid that Bill's farm would be deemed an unsuitable place for a teenaged girl. Mom had seemed far away on that drive home from Bill's, and her visits became more frequent after that day.

⚾ ⚾ ⚾ ⚾

But that was a while ago. On this day, all I knew is that my parents were oddly giggly about taking me on a drive. I ran upstairs to change, but not before seeing the conspiratorial smiles on my parents' faces as they sat together on the sofa. Something was definitely up.

Minutes later we were driving down a quiet country road with me on the front seat between them as though I were a young child. After crossing a rattling bridge with sturdy iron sides, Dad pulled off the road and parked at the end of a long black driveway that snaked up and around a farmhouse, then circled the outbuildings beyond. I'd seen the quiet farm before, not unlike the dozens I had drooled over on weekend drives through the countryside. Cutting through the gently rolling landscape was a wide stream that flowed along the front of the property beside a small orchard.

"That's Stemmers Run," Dad said. "I built a dam there for swimming when I was a kid and caught eels and sunfish under the old iron bridge."

The two-story, brown-shingled farmhouse stood in the afternoon shade of a towering willow tree. A flock of sheep grazed peacefully to the right of the driveway beyond a stone wall. It was like a picture on a calendar.

"How would you like to live here?" my father asked, turning to me, a grin spreading across his face.

"What?"

"It's ours!" he said. "Your mother and I just signed the contract."

"What? You bought a farm? *For me?*"

"Don't be silly," my mother said. "We bought a farm for our business and our family. See that bank barn?" She pointed to a sturdy structure built into the side of a hill and roughly the size of the house. "It's perfect for your father's business—plenty of space on the lower level for tools and electrical supplies and room upstairs for the men to gather for their assignments and materials."

"And that's a poultry building," Dad said, pointing to another large structure. "It would make a perfect stable. What do you think?"

I was speechless. Never in my wildest dreams had I pictured our family living in such a paradise.

⚾ ⚾ ⚾ ⚾

Renovations and repairs to the aged farmhouse took months, but there was nothing my clever parents couldn't do—plaster, paint, wallpaper, and install new hardwood floors. After we moved in, Dad gradually transformed the poultry building into a stable with a wide aisle and four box stalls—not to mention water and electric. Then we fenced in a pasture and a schooling ring. I continued visiting Bill's farm and Jet during our move and renovation process, grooming, cleaning stalls, and exercising the horses. Every day, I pictured Jet in my new roomy stalls and green pasture, but I knew that my parents could hardly afford to buy a horse on top of all the other expenses. Besides, Bill had always been firm about never selling his animals, saying, "These poor creatures have already had one bad break. They'll have a home with me until they die."

When our new stable was ready, I summoned the nerve to ask Bill if he would sell Jet and, if so, for how much. But he stood firm and refused to sell me the big gray horse. He did, however, *give* him to me on the condition that he could reclaim him at any time if I didn't care for him properly. This sent my mother into fits of laughter when I told her.

"That horse is going to think he died and went to heaven! And Bill is going to miss you a lot more than he'll miss that big horse's appetite! He has been exploiting your labor, you know!"

And then one day a neighbor stopped by and offered me a beautiful, quiet, mature bay gelding, free to a good home.

"Shaker is sound and a perfect beginner horse," she said. "I don't use him anymore, and I just need to know the old boy has a good home. He'd make a perfect stablemate to that gray horse in the field."

My mania was at an all-time high: horses before and after school whinnying to me from the field; horses in the quiet darkness before bedtime, and long summer days spent in the schooling ring and splashing through the stream. Nothing beat jogging over crisp autumn leaves on wooded trails or plowing through the winter snows on Jet. On Saturday mornings, there were riding lessons to neighborhood kids on the sweet, quiet Shaker. And on Sundays, the occasional horse show.

When Mom wasn't cheering for the Orioles or shouting obscenities at umpires, she was busy being lady of the manor—surrounding the house with flower gardens, tailgating at horse shows, attending the point-to-point steeplechase and the Preakness, dressing in tweeds, and so on. Most importantly, she always knew where I was. She had only one complaint.

"I don't like to see you ride cowboy style. It isn't ladylike!" What she meant, of course, was that the rich, refined people rode English, not Western.

"But Mom, Jet's strictly a pleasure horse. I can show him in more classes if I ride English *and* Western."

When Jet won trophies at horse shows, she displayed them on the dining room buffet beside her silver service—even when they were won in Western classes.

⚾ ⚾ ⚾ ⚾

It was paradise all right, until the evening my mother appeared at the stable door. I was reclining on Jet with my feet resting on his mane, working on my Spanish homework with Broadway show tunes playing quietly on the radio. Suddenly Jet lifted his head and pricked his ears forward.

"My, my," she said, looking around at the meticulous stable and gleaming tack room. "Your bedroom never looked this good!"

There was no pretense with Mom and me. She knew that I was as interested in polishing furniture and vacuuming as she was in soaping saddles and mucking out stalls.

She had all but given up on my domesticity—for now. As long as I maintained my grades, cut the grass, and did the weeding, she didn't bother me. Truth was, my mother liked to do things her own way. Her inner perfectionist was content to have me out of her domain, and I was more than happy away from her scrutiny.

Not that there wasn't plenty of grass-cutting advice. Who knew that mowing a front lawn required blueprints? It wasn't enough to make the grass shorter—oh no. The mower had to leave an aesthetically pleasing geometric design.

"People driving down Trumps Mill Road see our front lawn," she said at least once a week in the summer. "It's important to make a good impression!"

My mother's next statement as she stood in the aisle in front of Jet's stall sent me bolting upright, dropping my Spanish book onto the straw below.

"I've decided to take up riding. You can teach me on Shaker. I've watched you giving lessons. I know I can do it."

"But Mom, y-you have such a busy schedule." I didn't remind her she was in her forties. I was too busy picturing her riding beside me at horse shows, telling me what to do and how to do it. I knew it was all too good to be true.

Her mind was made up as she stepped into the stall and handed me my Spanish book.

"We can ride together! You can give me my first lesson tomorrow afternoon." She stopped at Shaker's stall and neatened his forelock and mane. He was lying down with Penny, my pet Rhode Island Red hen, perched on his withers.

"Oh look, she's laid an egg in the corner of the stall. Bring it in with you." She actually giggled as she left the stable, saying, "None of my friends know how to ride a horse."

I was puzzled. My mother had shown as much interest in

riding as I had in sewing draperies. Was she merely being lady of the manor and trying to impress friends? Or was she bored? Her energy was boundless. Besides housework and gardening, she played cards and had church commitments. And, of course, there was her real job in our new, modern basement office. Dad had offered to build her an office in his shop, but she preferred the comfort of the house. As the backbone of Dad's business, Mom spent countless hours behind the scenes. She was the equivalent of a modern office manager, CEO, and CFO rolled into one. Her toughness was invaluable. If a client missed a payment, Dad was—well—Dad.

"You never know," he'd say. "They might be going through a rough patch. We'll hold off and send another bill in a month or so."

Mom would listen patiently then pick up a stack of bills. "Carl, these bills are due now: three from the supply houses, one for college tuition, and one from the feed store."

Then she would bill the client again with a reminder that payment was overdue. If that failed to get results, she gave Dad moral support as he made those dreaded phone calls. Despite his non-competitive nature and lack of toughness, the business flourished. Church friends, Lions Club friends, and neighbors benefitted from his success and generosity when he hired their sons as helpers, giving them an opportunity to learn a skilled trade. Even an unemployed nephew came on board as an apprentice.

⚾ ⚾ ⚾ ⚾

Despite her *advanced* age (forty-something sounded so old to me back then), my mother was a quick learner and, before long, began joining me on the occasional trail ride. Naturally, she was dressed in my best show boots, britches, and jacket. Like everything else, these rides were always a production.

Just as Mom delivered freshly folded laundry to my bedroom, I delivered an impeccably groomed and saddled Shaker to the kitchen door. "Your mount, Lady Thelma," I'd say, handing over the supple braided reins.

One day she had my father take our photograph. It looked like the picture on our cookie tin of Queen Elizabeth and Princess Anne riding together on the palace grounds.

My mother, riding the handsome bay gelding, caused quite a stir as she led the way through the adjacent neighborhood to the trail. Women looked up from their sweeping and gardening, and children paused in their play to stare. In fairness, I never actually saw her wave like the queen. But then I wasn't always watching.

As it happened, my mother's foray into the equestrian world was brief. Our final ride together was that unfortunate summer day a man greeted us on the trail behind a construction site. I'd been whistled at before and was prepared to ignore him. As usual, Mom was dressed for the World Equestrian Games when the man waved—a bit too enthusiastically I thought. She was busy putting on her regal smile when he unzipped his trousers, dropped them to the ground, and flaunted the "family jewels," such as they were.

"Peggy, don't look!" she yelled, tightening her reins and picking up the pace. The last time I'd seen my mother with that horrified expression, we were taking a shortcut through the cemetery, and Shaker stopped to relieve himself on Victoria Van Keesler's grave. In panic mode, she had clucked to her horse and even dug her heels into his sides to get him moving.

"You're wasting your time, Mom. Shaker isn't going anywhere until he's good and finished." But she was busy looking around to see if anyone had witnessed the desecration.

The man at the construction site stood perfectly still, as

though he were posing for a statue (like Michelangelo's *David*). I took one last look as we moved off at a brisk trot and chuckled that my mother could even think I would be impressed. I cared for two male, thousand-pound horses, after all. This display was more reminiscent of the mushrooms that sprouted in the manure pile overnight following a rain. Sadly, I missed the expression on the man's face.

Mom discouraged me from riding the trails alone after that day, but she was way too busy to supervise.

⚾ ⚾ ⚾ ⚾

The next hiccup in paradise came on a January evening as we sat down to dinner.

"Honey, your father and I have a surprise. We're going to give you a sixteenth birthday party like we did for Janet."

Thanks to her optimistic nature, there was still some hope for another well-rounded, refined daughter, though I wasn't interested in boys yet and routinely ignored her pleas to participate in high-school social activities.

"Please don't," I begged.

"But it's a milestone. We should mark the occasion. Some families give young debutantes coming-out parties."

God forbid! "You took me to the National Horse Show in October, remember? Can't we call that my birthday celebration?"

In the end, she took pity on me and settled for an evening of culture instead. A world-class performance by Ballet Russe de Monte Carlo *was right up her* alley. As far as I was concerned, anything was better than a wretched dress-up party with boys and dancing—plus, she could brag about it later to her friends and family.

I was the compliant birthday girl on that January evening, seated between my parents in the orchestra section of the Lyric Opera House, with the aromas of Old Spice aftershave wafting in from the left and Tigress perfume from the right. One minute I was fascinated by the melodic orchestral tones and graceful ballerinas—the next, bug-eyed at the men's skintight costumes as they leapt through the air, defying gravity, while leaving little to the imagination. But for a thin layer of fabric and years of training (and some moral restraint), they could have been the man behind the construction site.

My mother was transfixed, immersed in her own little corner of *culture heaven* with an unfamiliar look of rapture. She was a world away from the Orioles fan who screamed at the umps and cavorted around the living room. The girl who had come to Baltimore from the country more than twenty years ago with a head full of dreams and a suitcase full of homemade dresses was sitting in the orchestra section of the historic, world-renown Lyric Opera House. It didn't get much better than that. She pulled the sequined shawl around her shoulders, threw her head back, and sniffed.

Dad was a different story altogether. Even in the dim light, I could see the pink creeping up his neck and onto his face. He stared down at his large, calloused hands until I wanted to hug him, but our family didn't indulge in such sentimentality. My parents showed their love for me a hundred times a day, but we didn't make a practice of hugging and kissing and saying, "I love you."

At home that evening, we had birthday cake and ice cream, and I received my real gifts—a framed photograph of my beloved Jet and a crocheted saddle blanket. The cake was devil's food, my father's favorite. He had earned every bite.

⚾ ⚾ ⚾ ⚾

Topper loved his new home. He'd taken to horse manure with the same passion he'd shown for the neighbors' garbage on Leslie Avenue. The gourmet delicacy in his own backyard was as delightful for rolling in as it was for snacking. He didn't show the same enthusiasm for the basement washtubs, though.

My longtime companion lived to a ripe old age and was laid to rest in a shallow grave on the hillside with a view of his favorite place: the manure pile.

Moving On

It was well past dinnertime when my mother flitted through the kitchen door and headed for the refrigerator.

"Good, you're not in the barn. Are you busy?"

I closed my World History book (grateful for the distraction) and braced myself for the daily third degree: *How were your classes today? Do you like your professors? Do you have a lot of homework? Have you made some friends? What will you be wearing tomorrow?*

It was more than curiosity about my new college life. She was a stage mother living vicariously through her daughter. She had even tried to accompany me to campus for freshman registration, just as she had taken me by the hand to first grade. In the end, she showed me how to write a check for my textbooks and sent me off on my new adventure alone. I knew that I was living her dream of a college education, but it felt like intrusion.

The year my sister graduated from college and settled down in her husband's home state of Virginia, I was a freshman at what was then known as Towson State Teachers College. It was just six miles from home, but light years away from my world—one where *diversity* had meant living alongside Catholics and Baptists. My new world included people of color, other faiths and ethnicities, gays and lesbians, and veterans.

My friends were other dayhops like me who ate brown bag lunches in the student center between classes. We weren't the cool coeds who went out for the cheerleading squad and dated jocks. There wasn't a homecoming queen or star athlete among us. Most of us had part-time jobs after class.

The career counselor in high school had suggested majoring in animal husbandry at the University of Maryland. "Your interest in animals and the out-of-doors is off the charts, Peggy!" he had said.

Seeing my mother's reaction, you'd have thought he had suggested a career as stripper on Baltimore's notorious "Block."

"Animal husbandry? What in the world would a young lady do with a degree in animal husbandry?" she asked.

"I'd work with animals. There are a lot of jobs out there. I'm good with animals."

"Nonsense! Animals are a hobby. Be a schoolteacher. You're a good Sunday School teacher and riding instructor. Children love you!"

I wasn't used to compliments from my mother. I was pretty sure I'd been a disappointment so far. I wasn't beautiful or brilliant or gifted, and I certainly hadn't distinguished myself or brought acclaim to the family.

In truth, it wasn't a surprise that my mother wanted me to be a teacher. She had mentioned it often. One time in particular stood out, when I was about nine years old. It was at Grandma Daisy's in Virginia, in the upstairs bedroom Mom had shared with her four younger sisters growing up. We were watching the sunset from the front window when, out of the blue, she recited a line from an essay she had written in her high-school English class all those years ago.

"In the evening, the setting sun paints a shimmering path across the quiet waters of the Great Wicomico River. My teacher told me, 'You have a flare for writing, Thelma!' " Then, with a faraway look, she said, "Someday you girls will go to college and become schoolteachers. Your grandmother taught school before she was married, you know."

I had no doubt that my mother could have been in charge of the whole world if she'd gone to college. But, despite the fact that she had read every book in the Fleeton Library at least twice and graduated from high school in the top of her class, college had been out of the question.

⚾ ⚾ ⚾ ⚾

There was a practical reason for my being at Towson. A state-wide teacher shortage in the late 1950s and '60s resulted in free tuition in exchange for a two-year teaching commitment in Maryland. Even with my part-time jobs and the occasional cash prize at horse shows, my parents could not afford horses *and* tuition. In the end, I was content living at home with my parents and animals and commuting to college.

But the third degree didn't come on this particular evening. Instead, Mom plunked a pile of fresh vegetables on the counter.

"You can make the salad. I'm running behind."

I drew in my breath. She was actually inviting me into her inner sanctum, the enchanted triangle between the stove, sink, and refrigerator where she plied her gastronomic magic. For me, it was the Bermuda Triangle, where my most recent disaster had involved a Blue Willow platter on a hot burner. I could still hear the sickening *crack* and see the blue and white chards poking through the sizzling sausages and eggs. It was the result of Mom's backfired attempt to show our visiting Virginia relatives my domestic side—Peggy, in an apron, at the stove.

But that was weeks ago, and, for my mother, life was about

moving forward. Each day was a fresh start, with past misdeeds forgotten. There was no time in her world for recrimination.

Like an Olympian passing the torch, she handed me the knife. "Don't cut yourself."

This was a first and should have been accompanied by music from a Wagnerian opera. My mother's mantra had always been, "If you want a job done right, do it yourself!" I thought about the ratcatcher blouse I'd made in my high school home economics class to wear in horse shows.

"You did a nice job on this collar!" Mom said when I brought it home. "I'm impressed." The following day, she took out both sleeves and sewed them back in correctly. I found no need to mention that my teacher had done the collar for me.

My mother poured a large bowl of leftover beef stew into a pot and adjusted the burner. I glanced up from my chopping to see her at the kitchen sink tying an apron around her slim waist, her lips moving in silent conversation. Something was up. Several months ago, I'd have guessed it was baseball, but the season had ended. For some reason, I felt a twinge of pity.

"Guess what? There are two women in my phys ed class who are older than you! You could still go to college if you wanted and be a schoolteacher yourself."

She laughed. "Are you kidding? I don't have the patience to be a teacher." She looked down at the chopped vegetables and frowned. "Those cucumber chunks and carrots are big enough to choke a horse. They need to be much smaller."

⚾ ⚾ ⚾ ⚾

My father was the official *prayer* in our family, and no one ate until the Lord had been properly thanked.

"Dear heavenly Father . . ."

The aroma of beef and onions and potatoes and carrots and succulent brown gravy made me dizzy with anticipation. Dad's prayers were reverent and relevant, heartfelt with no awkward pauses. When he filled in for our preacher at church, he wrote his own sermons, then Mom critiqued them. She sat in the front pew on those Sundays, her head held high.

"We ask these things in thy holy name."

He had no sooner said *amen* when my mother blurted, "I got a job today at Hutzler's department store!"

Mystery solved. Dad's broad smile mirrored hers as he shook catsup into his bowl of beef stew.

In typical self-absorbed fashion, I saw this as my big break. My mother was finally too busy to obsess on my activities, my grooming, my grades, my friends . . . not that she hadn't been helpful.

Earlier in the semester, I had developed a persistent case of conjunctivitis. I could barely open my eyes and fell behind in my American literature class. For hours, my mother lay beside me on the bed reading aloud. An avid reader, she devoured her Book of the Month Club selections and was a regular at the neighborhood bookmobile. Not ordinarily drawn to fantasy, she read the sentimental prose of *Rip Van Winkle* and *The Legend of Sleepy Hollow* with emotion and enthusiasm, and we laughed aloud together—just as we had enjoyed *Misty of Chincoteague* and *Black Beauty* years earlier. She had been right about animal husbandry, of course. I was happy at home with the people who loved me most in the world.

And now, my mother was going to be fully occupied in a job of her own. What a wonderful life it was!

⚾ ⚾ ⚾ ⚾

Hutzler's was a prestigious, upscale department store that had enjoyed a reputation of some prominence in Baltimore for a hundred years. Naturally, they would be impressed by my mother's authoritative, yet pleasant, demeanor. The fact that she had managed an office and dealt with the public was probably the clincher. And it didn't hurt that she was dressed more stylishly than her interviewers.

Mom was well-acquainted with current fashion and exclusive labels. She'd made it a practice to check out high-end shops before making purchases at more affordable stores or constructing a "knock-off" at home. Compliments on her chic outfits were as commonplace as A grades had been on my sister's report cards.

The world of retail fit my mother like her own custom-made garments. She left the house each day carrying a tote bag with her lunch and, during baseball season, her transistor radio. She had made friends with a seamstress in the backroom who joined her on these occasions.

Mom was bursting with excitement the evening she told Dad and me about the marketing idea she had taken to her supervisor.

"Our department displays dresses on mannequin torsos. Customers are always asking my advice on accessorizing, so I suggested displaying entire ensembles on full mannequins. You know: hat, purse, shoes, gloves, jewelry. Dresses would be more appealing, and what better way to advertise accessories?"

Her suggestion was implemented, and the results were an unqualified success. She took a personal pride in those stylish, inanimate figures looming throughout her department.

Before long my mother began assessing her current position and her prospects for promotion. She was as capable as her supervisors and had given them advice on more than one occasion. She made an appointment with personnel and was told, "We're pleased with your performance, Mrs. Knobel, and your job is secure. But Hutzler's policy is that, without a college degree, advancement isn't possible."

That settled it! It was time to find a career that rewarded ambition and hard work. On her final day of work, her seamstress friend took her aside. "Here's something for you, Thelma," she whispered, putting a stack of silky Hutzler's labels into Mom's tote bag. "We're using a new design and discarding these. I bet you can find a good use for them."

Soon after her departure from Hutzler's, Mom enrolled in a real estate course and found the career that was meant for her. Before long she was immersed in a world of listings, contracts, open houses, and settlements. My mother thrived on the office scene with its inevitable competition and interesting people. She left for work wearing tailored homemade suits with prestigious Hutzler's labels. Dad, always eager to follow her social lead, enjoyed get-togethers with their new friends. There were even afternoon baseball games at Memorial Stadium with colleagues who shared her passion and loved her enthusiasm. Go figure! Mom had her own dinnertime stories now, and we looked forward to them.

When she was called to list a house that was hopelessly cluttered or poorly decorated, there was no mincing of words.

"You'll never sell it in this condition!" she would tell the owner. "The odor of dogs and cats knocked me over when I came through the front door." Her penchant for honesty and openness proved an asset. Well, most of the time.

"You found the perfect place for some friends of ours and sold their house in two weeks," one young couple told her when she listed their property. "We want you to do the same for us."

A tour of their house was disappointing, and, at the end, agent Thelma handed them a to-do list.

"You need to invest in these improvements before putting your house on the market. It will be more appealing and increase the value."

They thanked her for her honesty and promised to call when they were ready.

Months later they kept their promise. With listing forms and high hopes, Mom entered the house.

"I hardly recognize it!" she said, looking around and mentally calculating its increased value and her commission.

"We did everything you suggested, Mrs. Knobel," the husband told her, proudly showing off the refurbished house.

"In fact," the wife said, looking apologetic, "we like it so much, we've decided to stay. It's exactly what we were looking for."

The strategy that had cost her two sales resulted in future referrals. As one of the top agents in her office, Mom eventually passed a million dollars in sales. This was a huge accomplishment in the 1950s and '60s.

⚾ ⚾ ⚾ ⚾

While my mother was setting the real estate world ablaze, I was keeping my head above water at college. The dean's list remained elusive, but Mom had been right about one thing: my supervising teachers called me a "natural" when it came to working with children.

The time had come to tell her about my new interest on campus, although she had probably guessed when I began curling my hair and raiding her closet.

Neither of us expected the storm that was on the horizon— one that came between us as nothing else had, not even baseball or horses or piano lessons.

New Territory

John was different from other boys I had met at college—boys who were away from home for the first time and giddy from an unfamiliar sense of freedom. There was none of that frivolity about John, who was an Army veteran taking advantage of the GI Bill. For him, college meant one thing: a career.

We met in physical science class when I was in my sophomore year and had absolutely nothing in common. I was cheerful and optimistic, Pollyanna-like, while John had that Eeyore, impending-sense-of-doom personality. His parents were divorced, and there were eight children in all—five from his father and mother and three more from his father and stepmother. Their exploits made my family look like we had stepped off the set of *Father Knows Best* or *Leave It to Beaver*.

There were no divorces in our family and few among our friends. I'd grown up believing that divorce was synonymous with shame and failure.

John had been working since he was a boy and on his own since his teens. In order to make ends meet in college, he worked at the post office and drove a school bus part-time. All this brought me face to face with a reality I had not previously acknowledged: I lived a privileged life. Not only had my parents indulged my passion, they were devoted and dedicated to helping me realize my full potential, whatever that might be.

I didn't mention my horses to John.

Preparing for class now involved more than completing assignments. Instead of pulling my hair back into a ponytail, I set it in soft curlers at night and wore it shoulder length. Finding attractive outfits was as simple as a trip to Mom's closet. For the first time in my life, I was dressing *for* a boy, not *like* a boy, and I was almost as pleased with the results as my mother.

Weeks passed, and when John didn't ask me out, I told myself it was just as well. My mother would find him unsuitable. A serious, older, worldly veteran, he would appear dark and brooding to someone so cheerful and positive.

And then one day out of the blue, I heard myself saying to her, "There's a student at school whose family lives out of town. I feel sorry for him—the cafeteria food is so boring. At least that's what everybody says. Could we invite him to lunch sometime?" I had tried to make him sound like a casual acquaintance, but as usual, my mother saw right through me.

"You should wait for him to ask you on a date first!"

"It's not a date. He can't afford to date."

I regretted my words immediately. I'd made him sound hopelessly poor and given my mother another teachable moment.

"You can fall in love with a rich man just as easily as you can with a poor one. Don't settle."

"But Dad was poor when you met him."

This was a mistake, as now I had to listen to her favorite story again, but telling it always seemed to put her in good spirits.

"It was the Depression; everybody was poor. There was no money for a wedding, so your father and I had no choice but to elope to Elkton. We recited our vows in a stuffy little wedding chapel before perfect strangers. Our reception was at a hotdog stand on the way home. I want more for you!"

"Mom, it's a simple lunch."

In the end, she agreed. I obsessed over every detail of the "simple lunch." Luckily, baseball season was over so John wouldn't see the crazy lady bouncing off the walls and throwing underwear at the TV. Madness can be hereditary, after all. It would have to be a Sunday afternoon when Mom didn't have one of her open houses for work, because cooking dinner myself could result in a very short relationship, if not food poisoning. Pot roast and home-made apple pie, followed by a walk along the rock garden path where a spectacular orange pumpkin lay in a tangle of autumn weeds. Then maybe a stroll through the orchard where limbs drooped from the weight of pungent, ripe apples and a visit to the stream bank where no male could resist skipping stones. Dad and I had passed many a happy hour along Stemmers Run doing just that. I loved his stories about smoking under the bridge at the age of eight and building a dam for swimming.

Then my casual friend and I would wander through the pasture where my four-legged family munched lazily on fall grass. He would see how gentle they were and insist on taking a ride.

"Oh!"

I could hear the disapproval in my mother's voice as I came down the stairs.

"You should wear a skirt for your date. Your pink outfit's in the closet. You look nice in pink."

"It's not a date, remember? And we'll probably ride afterwards." I had requested a casual lunch in our cozy, knotty pine kitchen, but my parents had stayed in their church clothes and the dining room table was set with Mom's Noritake china and Stieff Rose silverware.

"I begged her not to get fancy," I told Dad.

"Oh, you know how your mother likes to 'put on the dog.' Let her have her fun."

Naturally, I had withheld certain details about John—like his parents' divorce, as well as other aspects of a dysfunctional home life. I'd have to guide the conversation carefully.

My parents were gracious hosts that Sunday afternoon, and talk flowed pleasantly. Until Mom got down to brass tacks.

"Peggy tells us your parents live out of town, John."

"Well, my mother and her husband and his children live in Florida, but my father and his wife and their three sons are in Aberdeen. The five children from our original family in Cecil County have left home. They're all married except for me."

Mom had long since stopped chewing, and her eyebrows were nowhere in sight.

"Here, John, have some more pot roast," I said, my words coming at roughly the same tempo as my heartbeat. "You won't get anything like this in the cafeteria."

But Mom had picked up the scent. And I knew she wouldn't give up until she had run it to ground. "I . . . I guess you don't see much of your mother," she began, before John interrupted.

"This is delicious, Mrs. Knobel. The cafeteria serves SOS on Sundays."

"SOS?" she asked.

I jumped in quickly before John could elaborate. "Just because I'm not wearing an apron doesn't mean I didn't cook this meal," I told him.

"Did you?"

Dad choked and reached for his iced tea.

"Well, no, but I'm capable of preparing a meal."

This time my father's eyebrows mimicked my mother's. "If you like sandwiches," I confessed.

"Have you ever ridden a horse, John?" Dad asked, when his coughing had subsided and his breathing returned to normal.

"No sir. I've never cared for horses. I doubt that I ever will."

His statement was accompanied by emphatic headshaking indicating *end of subject*!

Dead silence. I looked down at my plate. I'd hardly eaten a bite, and John, with his left hand resting comfortably on the napkin in his lap, was finishing second helpings. Desperate to change the subject, I went with something safe.

"Did I mention that John is a history major?"

"Oh, really?" Mom's voice dripped with sarcasm and had a triumphant tone. "History is Peggy's least favorite subject. She barely passed last semester."

John's jaw dropped, and he turned to me in disbelief that anyone in her right mind could possibly not love history.

My stomach felt like Grandma Daisy's butter churn, and I was suddenly exhausted, as though I had run a marathon. What had I been thinking? Like the day I had run from Miss Blevins's classroom, I found myself without a plan. I returned John's stare and nodded my head emphatically.

"It's true," I said. "I've never cared for history. And I'm pretty sure I never will!"

Despite the disastrous conversation at lunch, our first non-date had broken the ice. When John left, I walked him to his car.

"By the way," I said, "Early American history is okay, I guess."

There was a hint of a smile as he turned the key. "And for the record, sandwiches are okay."

It was probably best that John had avoided my horses that day. He might have behaved like most boys inexperienced in horse etiquette and said stupid things like, "Hi-yo, Silver!" or "Giddy-up!" or "How do I make it rear up like Trigger?" Some behaviors are just too egregious to overlook.

$\otimes \otimes \otimes \otimes$

I hadn't expected my mother to embrace John unconditionally, but I had hoped she would be positive. Sadly, she showed only disdain for my friend and was barely polite when he picked me up for a real date, and then another.

There was a hint of desperation in her litany of disparaging comments to me that was out of character.

"He comes from a broken home, Peggy! That damages a person! He isn't happy. He never smiles! You two are exactly the same height. You can't wear high heels. You won't be stylish!"

When I came in from riding, she pounced with the force of Hurricane Hazel, which had caused Stemmers Run to overflow its banks four years earlier and deposited a dead pig onto our lawn.

"John doesn't like horses! You have nothing in common!"

The day she resorted to, "John drives like an old man," I knew that she was running out of ammunition. Mom was always on the warpath about people speeding in the narrow driveway that hugged the house as it wound around to Dad's shop. More than once, she had thrown down her tea towel and charged after a vehicle to admonish the driver, usually one of Dad's younger employees. John, ever cautious, crawled along the driveway at a snail's pace.

He felt the sting of her disapproval.

"I'm not coming to your house anymore," he told me one night as we sat in the car after seeing a movie. "I know when I'm not wanted." The song "Two Different Worlds" was playing on the radio.

"You're wrong. You know how mothers can be."

"She doesn't like me. That's not going to change."

"I'll talk with her."

"Don't bother. Maybe she's right. Like the song says, we're from two different worlds."

Weeks passed, and other than an occasional sighting on

campus, I didn't see or hear from John, and I was furious with my mother. She'd spent years complaining that I was too focused on horses when I should be socializing, going to dances, dating. And now that I was doing just that, she wasn't satisfied.

Open rebellion, the path my peers would have chosen, had never occurred to me before, but I was angry and, for the first time ever, stood up to my mother. Sort of.

"You know, it isn't John's fault that his parents are divorced or that he's not built like Wilt Chamberlain."

Mom's eyebrows shot up, and her jaw dropped.

"Besides, I'm not interested in any boy who laughs all the time. I guess you want me to date somebody who . . . who drives like a maniac!"

"Don't be silly! Your father and I just don't think he's suitable. He's six years older than you, and you said yourself he has been on his own for ten years. He was in the army, for goodness sake. You've never even been away from home!"

"I have so! Have you forgotten that I was a camp counselor last summer?"

It was a weak argument, and we both knew it. I had been as homesick as I was on the first day of school. It was the longest eight weeks of my life, and I'd begged my parents to drive the twenty-five miles to bring me home on my day off each week. Not only had I missed my horses, truth was, at the age of nineteen when most girls dreamt of being on their own, I had missed my home and my parents. I complained that my mother was bossy and domineering, yet I didn't want to be away from her.

But that was before I met John. I was a different person now and felt as though I had crossed a line. I wondered if things would ever be the same between my mother and me.

⚾ ⚾ ⚾ ⚾

A week before my summer retail job at Hutzler's department store was to begin, I still hadn't heard from John. At school, he barely acknowledged me, and at home, I treated my mother with the same detachment.

When Aunt Mary called and invited me to Virginia for a week, Mom encouraged me to go. I was shocked.

The youngest of my aunts, Mary was a free spirit. So much so that it was hard to believe she and my mother were sisters. When Mom spoke of her, it was often with a tone of disapproval.

When my aunt began asking me questions about John, I put two and two together. She had been given an assignment—to take my mind off an unsuitable suitor.

Despite my anger and resentment, it was a good week. I enjoyed my young cousins and aunt who believed that having fun should take precedence over work. They lived above my uncle's country store, and there was little that was regimented or even organized about Aunt Mary's life. It was like visiting another planet. I loved how her refrigerator was jammed with duplicates and triplicates of identical items from the store below. I loved how opening cabinet doors unleashed an avalanche. Aunt Mary never once said, "There's a place for everything and everything in its place!"

Most of all, I loved how clean laundry was thrown into a large closet and the ironing was done on a need-to-wear basis. At home, the sun didn't rise if the washing wasn't done on Mondays and the ironing on Tuesdays.

There was a goodwill about Aunt Mary and a welcome sense of freedom in her home. I envied my cousins. Aunt Mary was excited about the blind date she had arranged for the third night of my visit and insisted that I should be smoking a cigarette when he "set eyes on me" for the first time.

"Believe me, Peggy, you will look so sophisticated with a cigarette in your hand. Here, let me to show you." She chuckled and looked at me over her glasses. "Now don't you dare tell Thelma!"

I was rusty. It had been years since my rebellious days on Leslie Avenue. The filtered Winston was a vast improvement over Dad's Lucky Strikes. Aunt Mary draped my arm seductively over the back of the sofa and arranged my fingers just so.

When my young cousins giggled, she looked at them. "All right, you little fart blossoms, behave yourselves."

We hit it off, the recent college graduate and I. There was a bike ride, a swim party, and a Saturday night dance at the beach. He was nice and fun.

But he wasn't John. Still, when I left, future visits were planned—not quite what my mother had in mind.

At home, I missed John every day. Not even the horses helped. Over the coming months, Mom became impatient with my frequent weekend trips to Virginia on a Greyhound bus. Sometimes I caught her staring at me.

Serves you right, I thought. *Your little scheme backfired, didn't it?*

And then one afternoon, after I had traveled to Virginia two weekends in a row, a miracle happened.

"I was thinking," my mother said. "Maybe we weren't being fair to John. We're just worried that you don't have anything in common and he doesn't seem like a very happy person. And he's so serious."

"Oh, I can make him happy; I know I can. He was smiling way more than when we first met."

"But can he make you happy?"

"He already does. I hate high heels!" I almost told her about that day in physical science class shortly after we'd met. He sat directly behind me, and instead of pulling my hair like Tom Sawyer, he suddenly tilted my chair back until my head almost touched the floor. I screamed, and everyone laughed, including the professor, who was a friend of John's. It was uncharacteristically playful for him, and I was smitten. But I couldn't tell my mother that. It sounded silly, so I went with, "There must be something you like about him."

She was quiet for a few seconds. "Well, he does have impeccable table manners." Then, almost smiling, she said, "And he seems to be a sensible driver."

I wanted to hug her, but, of course, we didn't do such things.

⚾ ⚾ ⚾ ⚾

That Christmas we were engaged—a serious Army veteran who read history textbooks for pleasure and drove like an old man, and a cheerful young woman who pitched manure and galloped bareback across the countryside. Once when we were kissing goodnight, John suddenly reared back.

"Hold on a second! Am I kissing lips that kiss a horse?"

"It's all right," I assured him. "Jet and I have an understanding."

John worked for my father that summer as an electrician's helper. Late one Friday afternoon as he and the other workers were returning to the shop, I rushed out the back door.

"Oh no you don't, missy," my mother called after me. "You're not going out there and parade in front of those men!"

"What? I'm just going to say hi to John."

"It wouldn't be proper! John is at work. You'll see him later."

It wasn't surprising that she would use the word *proper*. She had always weighed behavior on a Victorian scale of propriety.

Now what kind of a twenty-one-year-old woman lets herself be bullied by her mother? I asked myself. I could have rebelled, but things had been so peaceful, I didn't dare rock the boat.

The closest we ever came to a mother–daughter talk was one winter evening in 1960, after my engagement had been announced in the Society section of *The Baltimore Sun*. I was sitting at the bathroom mirror wrapping my hair around curlers and admiring the sparkle of my new diamond ring when my mother came in and rearranged things on the vanity. When she began clearing her throat as though she were about to address the monthly meeting of the Overlea Lioness Club, I knew something was up.

Oh please! I thought. *Not the talk!*

"I don't approve of long engagements," she blurted, lining up the hand mirror with the comb and brush. "Things can happen . . ."

"Don't worry, Mom. We won't do anything foolish. I promise."

"Ha! That's easy for you to say, but men are interested in only one thing."

Surely, she wasn't talking about my *sainted* father. Our eyes met in the mirror and her eyebrows shot upwards, as though affirming some universal truth.

"I know what you're thinking," she said, wiping invisible spots from the mirror with her apron. "But it's true! Things happen. Things you haven't planned on that will change your life forever!" She sniffed and walked from the bathroom before I could begin asking questions— questions that she wouldn't want to answer.

That's when I first suspected. She wasn't talking about John and me. Could it be? Was it possible there'd been a time when my proper mother had not been quite so proper after all? How I longed to hear the story, but, of course, that was as close as she ever came to confiding in me. Heart-to-heart talks, especially about intimacy, were not in my mother's makeup. Besides, to do so would have betrayed my father. Perhaps a youthful indiscretion had helped to make him the non-judgmental, accepting man we all loved.

My mother's *talk*, which had been more revealing than she imagined, had been accomplished without once using the word *sex*.

The things my mother warned me about didn't happen, but not because of *the talk*. Truth be known, I was willing—*anxious* even—to be promiscuous, but my honorable fiancé would not betray the respect and affection he felt for his future father-in-law.

Maybe one day I would tell my mother that John was probably the most proper person in our family, though I suspect she already knew.

When it came to organization, my mother was the equivalent of perfect pitch. A professional wedding planner could not have been more proficient. I might have been a necessary piece of the puzzle, but details like music, flowers, clothes, and a reception didn't interest me.

Guests described our candlelight service as tasteful and elegant, just as Janet's had been four years earlier. She was my beautiful matron of honor, and John's brother, his handsome best man. Naturally, my four-year-old nephew, Stephen, stole the show as he carried our wedding rings down the aisle on a satin pillow and then sat on the carpeted steps to the choir loft twirling the pillow and looking bored.

Ours was a typical church auditorium reception—church ladies serving tea sandwiches and cake with nuts and mints. As the organist played my mother's favorite tunes on the piano, Mom smiled nostalgically, perhaps remembering an Elkton Wedding Chapel and a hotdog stand twenty-six years earlier.

For years to come, John's aunts and uncles would refer to our November wedding as the "dry reception." My mother was not in the least concerned about their stricken looks when they discovered that the fruit punch was just that—*fruit punch*. Billy Graham and the Mormon Tabernacle Choir could have officiated, and my in-laws would still have recalled only that there was not a drop of booze in the hall.

Before we left on our traditional Niagara Falls honeymoon, my mother took my new husband aside and spoke confidentially. I was curious and wondered if she was divulging what I had shared with her that afternoon as she fastened the dozens of buttons at the back of my satin wedding gown. It was an uncharacteristically intimate conversation for us.

"I got my period this morning," I told her.

I knew immediately that I'd made a mistake. I felt her stiffen, and as her eyebrows shot up, I was eight years old again and feeling her disappointment in me for leaping over the birdbath.

"Peggy! This is your honeymoon! You should have planned better!" I had failed at my only responsibility of the day. Her familiar flash of anger and disappointment was short-lived, and seconds later she stepped back and glowed.

"Oh, honey, you look so beautiful."

"Well, are you going to tell me what my mother said to you?" I asked my husband when we were finally on the road.

He smiled. "It was very sweet, actually. She asked me to be patient with you. Her exact words were, 'I'm afraid Peggy doesn't know much about housekeeping.' "

We laughed out loud, knowing that she had spoken God's truth.

In 1960, wedding nights were supposed to be a time for firsts. Ours was no different. It happened on the Pennsylvania Turnpike when the bridegroom, who drove like an old man, got his first speeding ticket—ever.

I couldn't wait to tell my mother.

Up in Smoke:
Marriage and the Family

John and I were still adjusting to married life when the call came from my mother.

"Are you ready for company yet? Your father and I want to visit. How about Sunday after church? We could come for lunch."

I couldn't speak.

After two months of marriage, I was still figuring it out in the kitchen. John was easy to please and amazingly tolerant of my culinary failures. I had a chipped tooth to show for my first attempt at cookies. Even the birds had turned up their beaks at my offerings. Fortunately, we were young and healthy with a high tolerance for poor cooking.

Keeping house was a breeze. A little mopping, a little dusting, a weekly trip to the laundromat.

"There's nothing to it," I told John. "I don't know why my mother makes such a fuss."

The pre-Civil War stone mansion was the perfect setting for a Gothic romance novel—or for a couple of newlyweds. Large casement windows in the living room of our second-floor apartment opened onto a sprawling front lawn with enormous beech trees.

Ornate fireplaces adorned the living room, dining room, and bedroom. In the rear was Ellicott City's version of the Hundred Acre Wood in *Winnie-the-Pooh*, ours to explore on weekends. Except for an aging landlord downstairs, there was total privacy. And it was all ours, including the use of a downstairs telephone and utilities, for a breathtaking $90 a month—barely doable on a starting teacher's salary of little more than $4,000 in 1960. John had insisted on putting my salary into a savings account.

"We should get used to living on one salary. We won't always have two," he reasoned, ever practical in financial matters.

We didn't miss a television or radio. We were oblivious to the twenty steps leading up to our apartment, the creaking wooden floors, and a serious lack of water pressure. We discovered early on that the solution to cold, cavernous rooms was snuggling. In two months of married life, our only visitors had been the bats and pigeons that dropped in through the fireplace chimneys. They gave my husband an opportunity to play hero at least once a week as he dispatched them through an open window with a tennis racket.

"Oh. Oh, good," I said, trying not to sound horrified at the prospect of my mother judging my homemaking skills, or lack thereof. "I-I was going to invite you. I've just been so busy getting my classroom up and running."

I was teaching third grade in the school where I had done my student teaching and still feeling my way.

"So, Sunday after church?" Mom asked. "I'm anxious to see those new pots and pans in action."

"Sure . . . uh, *this* Sunday?"

I pictured the unopened boxes in the corner of the living room.

"Is two o'clock all right? Your father and I have a meeting after church. Sandwiches will be fine. I'll bring a cake."

⚾ ⚾ ⚾ ⚾

"The nerve!" I said to John. "Like all I know how to make is a sandwich! I'm surprised she didn't tell me what kind!"

"Technically speaking, hamburgers and hotdogs are sandwiches," he said. "You've pretty much perfected those."

"That settles it! How difficult can a pot roast be, anyway? I've seen hundreds of them on our table at home."

John chuckled softly.

It was the end of January, and I convinced John to build our first fire for the occasion.

"We'll have dessert in front of the living room fireplace. My mother will be so impressed!"

While John set off to the woods for kindling and logs, I washed my new roasting pan and arranged a colorful halo of carrots, onions, and potatoes around the beef. Sandwiches, indeed!

At 1:15 P.M., John lit the match that would announce our presence to all of Ellicott City, Maryland. I finished setting the table with our sparkling china and silverware, then joined him in the living room.

"Oh, isn't this nice!" I exclaimed as warm flames danced in the mirror on the wall opposite the fireplace. "Entertaining is fun! I don't know why I was worried."

We were hugging when sirens sent us running to the front window.

"Fire engines are coming up College Avenue," John said. "It must be close!"

When the blaring sirens and flashing lights turned into our driveway, we spun toward the fireplace. All was well.

Banging on the front door sent us flying down the stairs, expecting to see our landlord on fire in his library. It wouldn't be the first time he'd fallen asleep with a beer in one hand and a burning cigarette dangling from the other. He was standing in the spacious foyer in a rumpled robe looking bewildered.

"What the hell? Are you cooking again, young lady?"

"Your chimney's on fire, sir," the fireman announced calmly. And then he made the understatement of the century. "I'm afraid you're gonna have a bit of a mess."

In no time, men with hoses scrambled onto the roof as years of creosote buildup burned in the flu of our living room fireplace, sending flames skyward.

Water cascaded down the chimney and into our living room, splashing wet ashes into the air.

We were frantically fanning smoke through the windows and trying to catch water in buckets when my parents appeared at our apartment door.

"Are you all right?" Dad asked John, whose entire face looked like Ash Wednesday.

"Do I smell dinner?" my mother asked, waving her hand in front of her face.

While the men dealt with the mess in the living room, Mom and I adjourned to the kitchen for the second disaster of the day. Lifting the lid to the roasting pan revealed the same arrangement I'd left an hour earlier—reddish meat, firm potatoes and onions, and carrots standing at attention.

"But, where's the rich brown gravy? It's been in here over an hour. Maybe the oven's broken, although it feels hot." I didn't mention that I was using it for the first time, or that it had taken both of us to figure out how it worked.

"A pot roast this size takes several hours! Don't you remember how I always put it in the oven before we left for Sunday School and church?"

I had never been aware of anything in the kitchen, and she

knew it. So, there it was. I was officially a failure in the kitchen.

My mother lowered her voice and spoke in a conspiratorial tone. "Get us some sharp knives and the cutting board and that big cook pot Elvira gave you at the shower. We'll make a pot of beef stew in no time; it's your father's favorite."

With slumping shoulders, I headed out of the kitchen while she called softly, "You picked a good cut of beef, honey. It'll be nice and tender."

Mom giving orders and saving the day, the story of my life.

By the time we sat down to dinner, the smoke had cleared, the mess in the living room had been cleaned away (except for the black ashes clinging stubbornly to the high ceiling), and our coughing had subsided. With the windows closed and the temperature rising, Dad paid me the ultimate compliment.

"This is delicious, hon! I'll have some more. It's as good as your mother's."

"Well, actually," I began, but Mom interrupted me, nodding vigorously.

"I told her that good stew is all about choosing the right cut of beef. She picked a good one." John winked at me.

I knew my mother. She'd be on the phone bragging about her daughter's delicious meal as soon as they got home. Of course, fire and smoke and ashes wouldn't make it into her story.

⚾ ⚾ ⚾

Thanks to that cold winter, I came to motherhood the following year, in 1962, with all the experience two horses, two dogs, and a cat could provide. My mother insisted on coming across town to stay with us for a week after the birth.

"Changing a diaper is trickier than pitching manure, you know."

"It really isn't necessary, Mom. Have you seen this?" I pointed to the nursery wall and my framed Red Cross Baby Care Certificate. "Remember that class I took last Saturday?"

"Oh, yes. Seven whole hours."

I know sarcasm when I hear it, so I put on my mother-of-the-year face.

"I changed a baby's diaper and bathed him." I didn't mention that it was a doll baby.

She had made up her mind so, in the end, I humored her, knowing that she couldn't wait to get her hands on her soon-to-be-born grandchild. And because I had left out the part about the doll slipping through my soapy fingers and bouncing on the floor like a rubber ball.

As it turned out, giving birth wasn't quite as easy as Princess had made it look in the barn. Perched on a mound of yellow straw, she had purred throughout the ordeal, pausing to lap a saucer of milk between kittens three and four. But then her babies weren't nine-and-a-half pounds!

After four difficult days, I was grateful for help. Mom took charge as we left the hospital.

"I'll take the baby."

"I'm sorry," the nurse told her. "We have strict orders to place baby in mother's arms in the back seat of the car." I couldn't see Mom's face, but I knew where her eyebrows were.

It was long before infant safety seats and holding my baby, Mike, in our car that day was like sliding onto Chico's furry back all those years ago. We were the only two creatures on earth, and for a while, I even forgot the pain of episiotomy and the raw soreness from nursing.

At home, I sat on a soft rubber ring feeding my ravenous baby boy while delicious aromas wafted from the kitchen. With my mother at the helm, our apartment took on the appearance of a decorator's showcase, with wedding gifts finally unpacked and tastefully displayed. Sometimes when she thought I was resting, I would peek into the nursery to see Mom rocking her sleeping grandson.

"I think Mom's as pleased with our baby as we are," I told John when we were alone.

"She's just relieved you didn't name him Trigger." John's sense of humor was coming along nicely.

Our engagement had brought an end to any negative comments about John, and, as was her nature, my mother had moved on to only positive thoughts.

⚾ ⚾ ⚾ ⚾

"It's best that I had daughters," she told me one day. "I'd rather deal with sons-in-law than daughters-in-law."

She was probably right.

Mike was Mom's third grandson, so she was a pro. I didn't correct her when she failed to use the Red Cross preferred method for holding our baby during his bath. But when she snapped a pair of rubber pants over his cloth diaper, I had to speak up.

"The Red Cross nurse told us never to use rubber pants on our newborn. They can cause diaper rash." It wasn't often I got to tell my mother what to do. Frankly, I was surprised she wasn't aware of that. She smiled patiently and removed the hazardous garment.

Changing our baby's diaper now meant changing his outfit, as well as the crib sheet, blanket, and clothes I wore while nursing him. Twenty-four hours later, the apartment smelled like a cheap nursing home. The following day, as John headed for the laundromat again, my mother snapped the rubber pants back on—and I kept my mouth shut.

When it was time for her to leave, I put on a brave face.

"You'll be fine," she assured me. "Oh, you'll make plenty of mistakes, all right, but look on the bright side. Your animals all survived, didn't they? And you know my number."

⚾ ⚾ ⚾ ⚾

Life was good, with one exception—my parents were selling off some land, the part with the stable and pasture. After my year-long teaching career, John and I were down to one salary, and the horses that I had little time for were a drain on our budget. Bill's words rang in my ears: "Most people can't be trusted to care for animals. No matter how good their intentions, they'll let the animal down in the end."

With a heavy heart and my dream of a farm far off in the future, I visited the Humane Society. I saw a healthy herd of horses on hundreds of acres, with doting caretakers. The manager, Bill's friend, promised to give my horses a good home, using them only for children's riding lessons on Saturdays. And the best part: "You can reclaim them whenever you're ready," she told me.

With Bill's blessing, we delivered my horses to their new home. As we were leaving, I thought about my old grapevine pony and how I hadn't given him a second thought after discovering the real thing. Was I now moving on from my horses to the real thing—a family? Would I forget about them? I hoped not.

Any guilt I felt over abandonment vanished when I visited through the years and saw a contented herd. I had mixed emotions when Jet preferred his four-legged friends to me. Shaker lived to the age of thirty, but I still looked forward to reclaiming Jet one day.

⚾ ⚾ ⚾ ⚾

Three years after our marriage came the bold move.

"Are you sure about this?" John asked over and over. "Do you really want to buy the house right next door to your mother? She'll be telling you what to do and how to do it—*every day*."

"I know. But the house is sturdy and affordable. There's land, a stream for our children to play in, and woods to explore."

"Hmm . . . and room for a stable and pasture someday." John wasn't born yesterday.

"Remember the last time your parents visited us? 'The inspector general is coming,' you said. You cleaned for a week and broke out in hives as they walked through the door."

"But they both work and have an active social life. They'll be too busy to bother us. They love their grandson. And those hives could have been diet-related."

My husband leaned close, looking deep into my eyes. "Your mother, every day—right next door."

"Free babysitting!" I said.

⚾ ⚾ ⚾ ⚾

For my mother, who was a foot soldier in the battle against dust and clutter, visiting our house was a walk on the wild side.

Seven-year-old Mike was reading a book to two-year-old Phil the summer morning Mom popped in on her way to the office. I was sitting at the coffee table in jeans and a baggy shirt helping four-year-old Scott with a jigsaw puzzle when she appeared through the porch window.

"It's the mothership," said Scott, looking up from the puzzle.

I sat up straight, smoothed my wrinkled shirt, and neatened my ponytail, wondering briefly if Scott was watching too much *Lost in Space.*

To her credit, my mother never openly criticized my house-keeping skills. Her approach was a bit more subtle.

"Hmmm. It must be nice to have all your housework done," she said, taking in the chaos.

While Phil looked at me and asked, "What's housework, Mommy?" Mom nudged Caesar the cat out of the way and gave Missy her traditional greeting.

"Nice doggie . . . now go away. Are you finished with this pile of blocks?" she asked.

"That's the Washington Monument, Nana," said Scott.

She walked around the national landmark, then lifted the skirt of her smart business suit (with the prestigious Hutzler's label sewn inside the collar) and stepped over a Lincoln Log village.

Then she gathered up several small toys from the floor and deposited them in the playroom/den, saying as if to herself, "There now, that wasn't so hard, was it?"

I grimaced, as I always did when Mom caught me relaxing. This wasn't the way she had raised her daughters, for sure. I couldn't remember a time when our living room was cluttered with toys while my mother was sprawled on the floor with her girls. If she thought I was lazy, she never actually said as much.

"What in the world do we have here?" she asked, throwing her hands in the air in mock surprise as she stared into the dining room.

The boys rushed to show off their latest collection of birds' nests, pinecones, and snakeskins.

"It's our science table!"

"We took a field trip to the woods!"

"We're going to the marsh this afternoon for frogs' eggs!"

"We're going to grow tadpoles like last year!"

"Hmmm, very nice. What is this?" she asked, picking up a round, prickly object.

Mike took a book from the table.

"It's called a seedpod, Nana. See? Here's a picture."

"It's from the sweetgum tree way back in the field," Scott chimed in.

"Did you wash your hands? I guess you know what poison ivy looks like," she said.

"Uh-huh," Scott said, putting his left foot up on the dining room chair and pointing to a red rash on his leg. "It looks like this. The white stuff is called calamine lotion."

"Oh dear, try not to scratch it!"

My mother looked around her and sighed. "Well, it doesn't look like you're having company anytime soon. Which reminds me . . ." Finally, the real reason for her visit.

"The Beckleys are coming for pinochle this evening at seven o'clock."

This was code for, "Have the children pick up the sticks and toys from the yard by 6:30 P.M." She had an image to uphold, after all. Mom never had sons.

Award-winning real estate agent Thelma Knobel told her grandsons goodbye and, as she left for the office, turned and smiled at me. "Goodbye, honey." I told myself that it was her way of saying, "Maybe there's more than one way to raise children." I exhaled, grateful that she hadn't gone into the kitchen where two box turtles named Shelly and Myrtle roamed the linoleum floor like cattle on the streets of Calcutta.

⚾ ⚾ ⚾ ⚾

We had worried needlessly about Mom's intrusion into our lives. That's not to say she didn't call her grandchildren in from play to tuck in their shirts or wash their faces and hands from time to time—or to share a batch of oatmeal cookies warm from the oven.

We all especially loved grandmother #2. What fun it was when she poked her head into our kitchen announcing, "Ain't the beer cold!" It was the signature expression of her favorite Orioles broadcaster, Chuck Thompson. It meant that the Orioles had won a game. I loved when the children joined her as she paced the lawn during a stressful game, their arms outstretched as they made tiny circles on their palms.

By the time Dad and John had finished building a stable and fencing in a pasture, Jet, too, had passed away of old age at the Humane Society. Our sons ranged in age from three to eight and, though they didn't share my passion for horses, they did humor me from time to time and join me on a trail ride. Mom was usually on hand with a camera on those occasions, especially when the pony cart appeared on her lawn. Bragging about your family is one thing, but, as everyone knows, a picture is worth a thousand words.

⚾ ⚾ ⚾ ⚾

There was mutual respect between my husband and mother. Not that they always saw eye to eye. I was an observer on one such ulcer-producing occasion. Mom was having a bad day and probably expecting company that evening when she confronted John in a dramatic fashion.

"There are tractor parts and a pile of wood in the back of the shop! It's the first thing people see when they drive up the lane, and I want it picked up now! The place looks like a junkyard!" she said, sniffing and throwing her head back.

If Dad had been there, he'd have said, "Hon, we're in the middle of a project. We'll pick it up as soon as we're finished."

But John looked at my mother and said calmly, "I beg your pardon. Who do you think you're talking to, Nana? This is John. I don't talk to you like that, and I'll thank you not to take that tone with me."

My immediate coronary thrombosis soon gave way to gratitude that my husband stood up to my mother, in a respectful manner. The alternative would have been to hold onto anger and harbor resentment. No one understood this more than my mother.

⚾ ⚾ ⚾ ⚾

There were other dramas in the family compound. My mother's sixtieth birthday party, for example.

Joining us for the evening were my aunt, uncle, and one of my cousins. Aunt Elvira was the only one of Mom's siblings who had settled in Baltimore, and we were close, not only because she was sweet and kind, but because, from the beginning, my mother had reservations concerning my uncle's suitability as a husband and father. It was her duty as the oldest sister to keep an eye on things. And that she did.

Aunt Elvira didn't drive, and we had always included her and my cousins in our daytrips and church activities. For her sister's sake, Mom tolerated my uncle for evening card games and family gatherings, though her eyebrows worked overtime on such occasions.

My house might not have been as sterile as the rancher next door, where one could literally eat off the floor, but it passed muster on this particular evening and the animals were safely sequestered in the basement. Or so I thought.

I had slaved most of the afternoon over a hot milk pound cake with boiled fudge icing, my mother's favorite. After the gifts were opened, Mom and Aunt Elvira led the way to our newly enlarged country kitchen where the long harvest table was set with my best Blue Willow dishes. When they stopped dead in their tracks and Aunt Elvira gasped, I knew that the time I'd spent on the preparations had been worth it.

Until my mother screamed.

In the center of the table, between the cake and colorful fall arrangement, stood Caesar the cat. Sensing that time was of the essence, the nine-pound ball of gray fur was shaking boiled fudge icing from his hind foot and lapping cream from the pitcher as if the house was on fire and the flames had reached his tail. He took my mother's scream as an ominous sign and leapt from the table, at which point our indignant dog took up the chase.

As the boys herded the animals back into the basement, and Mom scoured the cream pitcher and scraped icing from the side of the cake, seven-year-old Scott uttered the words that would live in infamy:

"Hey look, Nana! You can eat off of our floor too—if you like dog food and cat fur!"

My Aunt Elvira, who was never judgmental of my house-keeping standards, covered her mouth and laughed so hard she got a nosebleed.

Bragging Rights

My mother was to bragging what Rembrandt was to a portrait, especially when it came to her five grandsons. So much so that my sister and I worried that our relatives would resent our "exceptional" sons.

The year our first-grader played a piano duet with his music teacher at the school Christmas concert, my mother's eyes sparkled with pride.

"Mom, it's only 'Chopsticks,' " I reminded her.

She sniffed and threw her head back. "I believe the announcer called it '*Christmas* Chopsticks!' " She returned her gaze to Phil, no doubt imagining his future as featured pianist with the Baltimore Symphony.

When the orchestra joined in, her smile broadened. Imagine! Her youngest grandson playing piano with a full orchestra, at the age of six. She turned to the stranger seated beside her. I couldn't hear her, but I was pretty sure she wasn't explaining that her grandson was banned from the chorus for not doing his classwork.

The evening my mother learned that Scott had scored the highest SAT grade in his high school, she went to her bridge game with a spring in her step. The summer day outdoorsman-Scott dove into the deep end of a pool and saved a drowning man's life, Mom took to her bullhorn. She overlooked her grandson's Dungeons & Dragons mania, keeping her disapproval to herself the Sunday Scott walked down the church aisle to a Bach prelude in his black jacket with a gold fire-breathing dragon on the back. It was the compromise my son and I had reached when he informed me that he didn't have time for church and reminded me of the day I walked this very aisle in a fringed suede jacket.

Of course, I never shared my own concerns about the role-playing game with my mother. There had been tragic stories in the news about Dungeons & Dragons fanatics. Nor did I tell her how I had stalked the group of five or six self-described *nerds* during their meetings and games in our basement. I didn't mention the times I had sat on the stairs listening as they lived vicariously through the exploits of their D&D characters. My presence would have been as welcome as my mother's when she stalked me at Triangle Farm and Bill's place.

The athletic and academic achievements of Janet's sons in Virginia were a source of great pride and material for Mom. If there were any negatives in their lives, nobody heard about them from my mother. The day would come when she would work into conversations that Gary was a college professor over in Washington and that Stephen and Scott were structural and civil engineers. "Imagine, a college professor and two engineers in the family!" she'd say.

Constantly on the prowl for material, Mom left no stone unturned. The year Phil had the lead in his high-school production of *Harvey*, something as mundane as a rabbit hopping across the yard could unleash a glowing critique of his Elwood P. Dowd portrayal. When he played the cowardly lion in *The Wizard of Oz*, Mom compared his performance to that of Burt Lahr.

My mother was an equal-opportunity bragger, proud of all her offspring. But when Mike's television career took off, she hit the lottery. Fans actually pursued the grandmother of the local TV personality.

"We saw your grandson on television this morning, Thelma. My, he has a nice voice."

"Oh, thank you," she'd say, giggling and waving them off, as though the subject were too embarrassing. "He and Scott sang in the church choir, and Mike sang with the Baltimore Opera, you know. I attended every performance."

The year Mike had a brief solo in the opera *Martha,* my mother hosted a pre-performance dinner party like the ones written up in the Society section of *The Baltimore Sun.* She invited certain relatives and a few friends with an appreciation for the arts.

Six months after Mike became a host on QVC, collectable dolls stared down from Mom's china closet, and her kitchen cabinets looked like a T-Fal warehouse.

Her QVC Diamonique pendant presented endless bragging opportunities.

When *Dirty Jobs* debuted, I was as happy for Mom as I was for Mike. Lord knows I had given her precious little to brag about growing up. I still remembered that Sunday morning on the church steps where a group of ladies stood talking about a school dance their daughters had attended the night before. I arrived on the scene in time to hear my mother's jaded voice.

"Well, Peggy's not much when it comes to dancing, but she sure can pitch manure!" She seemed pleased by the laughter. She had one accomplished, *normal* daughter to her credit, so there was no danger of her parenting skills being called into question.

At ninety-one, Mom had supported every step of Mike's TV career. His squeaky clean, wholesome reputation was a reflection of his roots. Naturally, she had told everyone she knew to tune in to the Discovery Channel that first Tuesday night at 9:00 P.M. for the show with the quirky little title, *Dirty Jobs.*

At 8:58, the phone rang. "Ain't the beer cold! Are you watching? One minute to go. I'll call you during the commercial," she said.

Suddenly, there he was, our son—or so we thought. It was difficult to recognize him in the rubber suit and breathing apparatus. He could have been a moonwalker had he not been standing knee-deep in guano, surrounded by blackness and deadly fumes. As urine and other bodily fluids from millions of bats rained from above, a biologist warned Mike that the guano was filled with dermestid beetles committed to cleaning the flesh from his bones if given half a chance.

At the first commercial break, John and I turned to each other with a frozen look of horror—our popcorn and soda untouched. When the phone rang, I jumped, then took a deep breath.

"Hi, Mom."

"Peggy!"

"What's wrong? Are you having trouble breathing?" I asked, worried that her congestive heart failure had flared up.

"Peggy, Michael's in a bat cave! He's standing in filth, with flesh-eating beetles!"

"Mom, you spoke with him yesterday. You know he's all right."

"He's on national television! Our family's watching! My friends are watching!"

I explained the concept of the show, again. "Mike works as an apprentice for a day with people who do the jobs most people don't want—jobs that make our lives more comfortable."

With each episode, she called during commercials and vented.

"Did you see where his hand was?"

"Your son said *holy crap* on national television!"

"Michael was drinking beer. Do you think that sends a good message?"

"Peggy, the next time you talk to Michael, remind him that

Peggy on Cindy

John and Peggy's house, 1990s

Phil, Scott, and Mike

Phil and Harvey

Outdoorsman Scott

Thelma's five grandsons: Gary and Steve Jones
and Phil, Mike, and Scott Rowe

Scott, Marjie, Katie, and Jessica Rowe (with Jasper and Lucky)

Mike, John, Thelma, and Peggy

Stephen, Janet, and Gary Jones

The Jones family: Stephen, Janet, Morris, and Gary

The Rowe family: Peggy, Scott, Mike, Phil, and John

The Rowe family's infamous Christmas portrait:
Mike, John, Scott, Peggy, and Phil

Scoreboard at Camden Yards, 2003

Thelma's major league pitching debut, 2003: Janet Jones, Gary Jones, Thelma, Scott Rowe, Peggy Rowe, Mike Rowe, Phil Rowe, and Katie Rowe

Thelma and Jim Palmer in the Orioles' dugout, 2003

Thelma with her prized autographed
baseball and Orioles hat, 2003

Baltimore Orioles'
mascot and Thelma at
the big game, 2003

Thelma Knobel

Regis and Kathie Lee could be watching. Good heavens, the Queen could be watching!"

Through it all, Mom's pride remained intact, especially when a well-groomed grandson appeared on talk shows or in commercials. The Tuesday night we saw Mike standing knee-deep in steaming manure, stripped to the waist with his arm up the rear-end of a bull, I let John answer the phone.

Our Christmas Close-up

I was heading for the mall exit when a stranger approached me and shoved something in my face. A similar incident had just occurred in the cosmetics aisle of a department store when a saleslady sprayed me with a nauseating perfume.

This time, a woman said, "Here you go, ma'am, a coupon for an 8x10 family photograph—absolutely free!" She spoke fast like a carnival barker.

I hated these wretched trips to the mall! Buying a gift for my mother was an impossible task. Christmas was so much simpler back in the good old days when she bought her own gifts, along with everyone else's.

Not again! I thought, raising my hand and turning my head away from the annoying woman. And then, as I swerved, she waved a coupon in the air and said something that got my attention.

"It would make the perfect Christmas gift, hon!"

Now, I've always been a skeptic when it comes to angels and such, but there was an unmistakable aura around that woman's head when she slapped the coupon in my hand.

The more I thought about the family portrait, the more excited I became. I stuck the coupon in my pocket and headed for the parking garage picturing the photograph of my sister's family that hung on my parents' living room wall. It was the first thing guests saw as they entered the house, and Mom regarded it with pride. Janet, wearing a classic, tailored dress and Morris and the boys in suits. The quintessential successful American family. The picture had always reminded me of the Cleavers—Ward, June, Wally, and the Beaver, though I never told my sister.

I started the car, picturing my own family photograph beside my sister's—John and I in our Sunday best, flanked by our three handsome sons wearing tuxedoes. They had been a frightful expense at the time, but, as members of their elite high school *a capella* chorus and concert choir, tuxedoes were mandatory.

It would be the perfect Christmas gift for my parents! Mom would probably hang one of those gallery lights over it.

By the time I reached the main road, reality was setting in. Who was I kidding? It would take more than a coupon to get my busy family in one place long enough to pose for a portrait. I stopped at the bakery.

It was one of those rare Friday evenings in our house when everyone showed up for dinner. When the time came, I placed the platter of éclairs in front of my four men and whipped the coupon from my pocket.

"Hey, look what we won, a free family photograph! It'll be the perfect Christmas gift for Nana and Pop."

"They already have a picture of our family," John said, wiping chocolate from his lips and pointing to the end table. "Like that one."

"Oh, that was taken when the children were young. You had all your hair and I was thin. See?"

"Exactly!" he said, taking a sip of coffee. My husband resisted anything new, especially things he regarded as frivolous—a touch-tone telephone, a microwave, a clothes dryer. If he hadn't gotten married, he'd be sitting on a crate, cooking squirrel over a bonfire.

"Did I mention it's free? The boys could wear their tuxes. Mom and Dad would love it. Okay guys, I'm desperate!" I yelled. "I'm going to make an appointment."

"Sorry, Mom, but I'm lifeguarding all weekend." Scott, our nineteen-year-old college sophomore, worked part-time at the Holiday Inn at the Inner Harbor.

"And I'll be out of town with the quartet," said Mike. At twenty-one and out of college, he still lived at home. I knew this because his dirty clothes surfaced in the laundry from time to time.

"It won't take long," I pleaded.

Sixteen-year-old Phil was easy. "I'm free anytime," he said, reaching for a second éclair.

"Come on, Mom, you have to admit that studio photographs are boring!" said Mike. To prove his point, he walked to the end table and held up our picture. "Look at us! Five mummies in the shape of a pyramid."

Scott chuckled. "We look like bowling pins with hair."

"I love that picture!" I said. "It was taken by a professional photographer."

"Exactly!" spoke the voice of reason.

"Now, if we could dress in character, that would be a different story." Suddenly Mike sounded enthused. "An expression of our personalities and interests—our *aspirations*."

I looked around at my family, picturing Scott dressed as a conscientious student, Mike as a young businessman, and Phil in something casual but tasteful. John and I would dress as respectable schoolteachers, of course.

"Well, as long as we all look nice," I said. "Nana has high standards, you know."

Mike picked up the coupon. "Here's a telephone number.

Maybe they can take us *now*."

"I just took my suit off," John grumbled.

"Great!" I heard Mike say a minute later. "We'll be there in an hour, and we'll be dressed a little unconventionally." He said goodbye and turned to us.

"Listen up, everybody. The studio has an opening in an hour. Dad, that undershirt's perfect. The little hole's a nice touch. Put on some suspenders and a cap. Take your pipe and the newspaper."

"Now you're talkin', son!"

My mouth fell open. "Your father is not going to dress like L'il Abner for our formal portrait!"

Mike shrugged. "That's how I see him, Mom."

"It's called realism," Scott explained in his sophomoric wisdom. John headed for the bedroom whistling.

"You're fine, Mom. Just keep that apron on, maybe smear some flour on your nose."

I was losing control.

"That's how we all see you, Mom," said Scott, mirroring his brother's enthusiasm.

"Come on, guys, let's get our outfits together," said Mike. "At least shave, Scott," I shouted up the stairs behind them.

Forty-five minutes later, we strolled through Golden Ring Mall looking like the Village People, except for John, of course, who was a hillbilly straight out of Dogpatch, USA.

The receptionist stood up and stared as we approached.

"It's okay," our son assured her. "I cleared it with the manager." In a small room, he posed us before a tripod. Across the hall, a photographer was arranging a neatly dressed family in the shape of a pyramid.

"Ah, the good old days," I reminisced. "I thought I asked you to shave, Scott," I said.

"I did. I used Dad's electric razor."

"You have to plug it in!" I said.

A second later, I stared up at my son, the flasher, wearing a red bow tie, his tanned hairy chest peeking through his raincoat.

"Now, wait a minute," I began, but he interrupted me.

"This is it, guys. Dad, give me a pensive look. Mom, a vacant smile—you know, like Edith Bunker. Scott, a rebellious, know-it-all grin. And little brother, I need a big carefree, fun-lovin' laugh from you."

From the corner of my eye, I could see Scott's headband and the message on his shirt: "Students of the World Unite!"

I should have felt gratitude that he wasn't smoking a joint and John wasn't drinking moonshine from a jug.

The photographer appeared, raised his eyebrows, and gawked. "Whoa! Is it Halloween or something?"

"This is what we want," said my husband, opening his newspaper. "This is definitely us."

Accessorized with an apron, a mixing bowl, and a spatula, I forced a toothy grin and knew at once the perfect spot for the photograph: my bottom dresser drawer.

A week before Christmas, we picked up our family portrait. Phil, the family entrepreneur, promptly entered it in a contest at a local store and won dinner for four at a posh restaurant in Columbia, Maryland. For Christmas that year, John and I gave my parents a box of Whitman's Assorted Chocolates (with cream centers), a bottle of White Zinfandel wine, and dinner at a posh restaurant in Columbia. They were delighted.

We treated Phil and Scott and their friends to dinner at a local "hamburger joint." They were equally delighted.

Our family portrait still hangs in a place of honor in our home. Mom smiled when she saw it, I think.

The Day Mom and I
Ate at the White House

My mother discovered day-tripping by bus when she was in her late eighties. She looked forward to these excursions with the same anticipation she held for Oriole games and Christmas. For my father, these bus trips were right up there with a stomach ulcer—with perforation. He put it succinctly: "There's too much eating and too much shopping! And my rear end can't take all that sitting!"

Mom understood. They had spent some wonderful winters together in Florida while Dad could still drive. And now her *love* should spend his twilight years doing what made him happy.

So Mom joined the local AARP group, which was filled with like-minded seniors. While she climbed aboard comfortable motor coaches for a day of adventure, Dad and John (now retired) climbed aboard the tractor and headed into the woods for a day of sawing and gathering firewood. With a thermos, a bag lunch, and two exuberant dogs in tow, they lived every man's dream—well, Dad's dream anyway. Oh, there was grass-cutting and the occasional home repair or improvement project, and, naturally, afternoon coffee at McDonald's "shooting the breeze" with other retirees.

I loved Mom's bus excursions, and not just because of the yummy bakery treats she carried home. My mother could still tell a good story, and senior bus trips were rife with drama. Whether the stories were completely factual or not, they were entertaining and often hilarious—and perfect for someone who loved the spotlight.

On one trip, a traveling buddy discovered that she had mistakenly discarded her false teeth with her trash at McDonald's on the way home. When she missed them, several miles down the road, she was so distraught that the driver, with forty seniors on board, turned the bus around and drove back. After the manager rifled through the trash with no luck, the driver insisted the woman empty her purse on a table. And there were her dentures, wrapped in a wad of paper napkins along with several creamers and packets of mustard and ketchup.

"She wasn't very popular on the trip home, I can tell you that!" Mom said. Funnier still was a trip to Winchester, Virginia. As the bus swayed and swerved around the Blue Ridge Mountains, the woman sitting across from my mother threw up into a small trash bag.

"And don't you know, after a while, the woman sitting beside her started filling up her own trash bag," Mom said, making a face.

"This is the best part," she said. "We were going around a mountain when a man came crashing through the lavatory door! He landed in the lap of the women across the aisle—with his pants around his knees!" she said, giggling. "I learned something today. *Never sit across from the lavatory!*"

She needn't have warned me; I had made up my mind long ago that, when it came to bus trips, I was with Dad. So when my mother invited me on a holiday bus trip to Washington D.C., I was ready with an excuse.

"Thanks, Mom, but I'm way behind in my Christmas shopping. I just don't have the time, I'm afraid."

My mother's persuasive tactics, though subtler in later years, had grown even more effective. Just as some artists prefer oils, and others watercolor, my mother's preferred medium was guilt—and she applied it liberally.

"But, honey, this is your Christmas gift to me. I'm almost ninety, and I've never seen the White House. This is my last chance. We should see it together."

Why couldn't I just say, "Mom, you have lots of friends. Invite one of them to go with you!" But her pitiful plea brought to mind a trip to Chincoteague all those years ago. She had done it for love and even managed to enjoy herself. I could do as much.

She resembled a Norman Rockwell painting that December morning. A sprig of holly in her permed gray hair, silver bells dangling from her ears, and enough enthusiasm to fill a bus. There was a light dusting of powdery snow on the grass when I dropped her off next to the two buses that were parked at the curb.

"You can get in line while I park the car in the back," I said. "Be careful!"

Minutes later I grabbed our tote bag, locked the car, and boarded the bus with the D.C. sign in the window. On board, I looked for my mother, but she was nowhere in sight. I ran to the front and told the driver she was missing. He immediately blew his horn to stop the bus behind us that was pulling away from the curb and heading north to Philadelphia.

Finally, after the nice driver retrieved my mother from the northbound bus, we sat side-by-side heading south to our nation's capital. I tried not to think about the decorations on my dining room table and the unopened box of Christmas cards.

"Isn't this exciting?" Mom said, her bells reflecting the morning sunlight and jangling when she moved her head.

"Yes, very exciting."

An hour later, we arrived at the White House.

"After the tour, you will exit on the other side of the building. Just look for our bus along the curb," our driver directed. "Enjoy yourselves!" I admired his Christmas spirit. It matched my mother's.

"Wait for me, Mom," I said, taking her scarf from the tote bag. But she was halfway down the aisle and out of earshot. I panicked when I heard, "Aw, that old lady fell."

By the time I reached my mother, the bus driver was on the sidewalk and helping her to her feet. "She's all right," he said to me. "She went down slow and landed easy." And then in a whisper, "You might want to keep your eye on her." Like I hadn't tried.

"Did you get wet, Mom?"

"No, I'm fine," she said, taking my arm. "Isn't this fun?"

Inside the White House, Mom paused at each room, drinking it all in with reverence and sounding like a docent until the guards moved us along.

"This was President Kennedy's favorite room," she informed me at the Blue Room. "This is the official Christmas tree," she said at the Red Room. "Isn't this a lovely shade of red! The color for the walls and upholstery was chosen by Hillary Clinton." My mother had clearly done her homework.

Our final stop was the East Room, where school choruses were singing carols before an enormous Christmas tree decorated with ornaments from around the world. Here, Mom called my attention to the famous portrait of President George Washington and looked sad when she spoke of Presidents Abraham Lincoln and John F. Kennedy lying in state in this very room. "Lynda Bird Johnson was married in the East Room," she told me.

Then she opened her purse. "Here," she whispered, pressing half a dozen Wheat Thins into the palm of my hand. "Munch on these. You can tell your friends you ate at the White House with your mother."

I stifled a giggle and kept an eye on the guard while we nibbled our crackers. People were enjoying, "Here Comes Santa Claus" when I looked around and didn't recognize anyone else from our bus.

"Uh oh, we have to leave!" I said.

"Not yet." Mom shook her head firmly. "President Clinton still might show up."

"Mom, the bus!"

She looked at me with pleading brown eyes. "I'll never get here again, honey." She looked toward the stairway, hoping for a miracle. After two more carols, I guided her from the White House and looked along the curb. There were a dozen buses, but not ours.

"There it is," my mother said, pointing across the lawn. "And it's driving away!"

"Oh, crap!" I said, panicking and mentally calculating the taxi fare back to Baltimore. I scurried off, waving my White House brochure in the air. Pigeons fluttered around me, and tourists stared.

Thanks to D.C. traffic, the bus had come to a standstill when the passengers saw me and alerted the driver. I hurried back for my mother. She was standing in the exact spot where I had left her, with her mouth open—as though she'd seen Hitler's storm troopers marching toward her.

"Peggy! You said *crap*!"

"I did? Well, I must have been extremely upset. Come on, we have to go. They're waiting for us."

In the bus, we were greeted by our driver's icy stare.

"Where have you been? Thanks to you two, we're twenty minutes behind schedule!"

"We were enjoying ourselves like you told us to," Mom said, matter-of-factly.

"I'm sorry," I mumbled, out of breath.

He wasn't smiling, and neither were the other passengers. "If this happens again, I won't wait. You'll have to take a cab to our next stop."

I sat beside my mother, feeling sorry for anybody who left her dentures in a restaurant today. Moments later, our bus pulled to the curb.

"You're on your own for a quick lunch," the driver announced. "Be back on the bus by one-thirty. *We're behind schedule.*" He was staring directly at me, of course. An old woman across the aisle tapped her watch and repeated loudly, *"One-thirty!"* Mom sniffed, raised her eyebrows, and threw her head back.

We slipped into a noisy café, popular with young people and famous for loud music. A busy waitress seated us at a round table with six strangers. We were halfway through our soup and shared sandwich when the other diners threw money into the center of the table and left. When we finished, the waitress was nowhere to be found, so we added our money to the pile and headed for the door.

We were almost there when a hysterical voice silenced the lunchtime hubbub. "They're getting away! Stop them!"

My first thought was that there must be a hold-up. I tried not to panic as I grabbed Mom's elbow and looked for something to hide behind. Throwing her under a table didn't seem like a good idea. Suddenly, our waitress appeared and waved a stack of bills in my face.

"You two stiffed me out of my tip!" she yelled.

Diners stopped eating, and people waiting in line stared at us as if we were making off with the till. I told myself I would never see these people again—except for those from our bus, of course.

A muscular young man with a shaved head and red bow tie stepped in front of us. His arms were folded across his chest, and he wore a gold earring. He was Mr. Clean without the friendly smile.

"You two owe me money!" the indignant waitress shouted in our faces.

"We left the amount of our check plus a generous tip," I said. "It was the others at our table . . ."

"No problem," said the man, flexing his biceps. "Just pay the waitress, then collect it from the others when you get to the bus."

The bus! I looked at my watch. 1:25 P.M. "Uh, how much?" I asked.

"I'll settle for ten bucks," said the waitress.

It was extortion, and I should have asked to see the manager, but it was worth $10 to get back on the bus by 1:30. As I opened my purse, Mom slapped her wrinkled, arthritic hand on top of mine and announced firmly, "Those people were not from our bus, young lady, and we're not paying somebody else's bill." She took my arm, and together we walked around Mr. Clean and through the quiet cafe. When we reached the door, there was scattered applause, which Mom acknowledged with a nod and a jingle.

"Isn't this a wonderful trip?" she said, taking my arm as we headed up the sidewalk in our nation's capital. "And didn't you just love the White House?"

I turned and stared at her, wondering where she had been for the last humiliating half hour—and that's when I saw them. The waitress and bouncer were right behind us, little puffs of steam coming from their nostrils and goosebumps on their bare arms.

"We'll see what your bus driver has to say about this!" the bouncer called to us.

I had the strongest urge to walk past our bus, but it was late, and Mom was tired, so I climbed the steps behind her.

"Well, well," said the driver, looking at his watch and smiling. "Look who's back almost on time."

I pointed over my shoulder. "These people say we owe them money, but we don't. It was those other . . ."

Suddenly, the Grinch stood up and put his hand on my shoulder.

"Just take your seats, ladies. This isn't your problem. I'll take care of it."

We sat down and looked out the window in time to see the waitress and bouncer turn on their heels and head back to the restaurant.

"Merry Christmas, dear," my mother said. "This is your best gift ever." Then she put her head back and closed her eyes. "Remind me to pick up some pastry at the restaurant. We'll have some good stories tonight."

"Two more stops," the driver announced: "The Arboretum and the National Cathedral. I hope you saved room for a big dinner at Mrs. K's Toll House Restaurant."

I rubbed my throbbing temples, wondering if today's drama would ever end. I knew I didn't have to worry about my *language transgression* being part of tonight's story. It wasn't the sort of thing my mother would repeat. By the time the bus began moving, Mom was snoring softly.

On the bright side, how many of my friends have eaten at the White House with their mothers? I wondered if someday I could find some humor in today's excitement. I doubted it.

The Rascal Scooter

It comes to us all in the end—that role reversal between parent and child. It's a natural progression. Unless, of course, your mother is the take-charge type like mine. Then you'd better stock up on Tums.

I dialed my mother's number at the retirement home, struggling to keep my eyes open. I had lain awake half the night, rehearsing my speech. It was time to tell my ninety-one-year-old mother she could no longer drive her motorized scooter through the hallways of the retirement home. There had been an *incident.*

I had gone through the same drama just a year earlier, when I had to tell her that she could no longer drive her car. Her response was seared in my brain.

"I'll know when it's time to stop driving! Nobody will have to tell me!" Her expression said, "Who do you think you are, giving me advice?" And I was twelve years old again, being told to go to bed because it was a school night.

"Mom, you don't need to drive," I had told her. "There's a shuttle bus, and I'm available most days." She sniffed and threw her head back.

"Mom, you fell asleep behind the wheel! Remember?"

"I was in the parking lot, for Pete's sake."

"Mom, your door was open, and you had one foot in the car and one foot out. Security thought you were unconscious!"

It took months and cost me a fortune in Tums, but I finally convinced her to sell her car.

That was a year ago, and now I had to tell her that she could no longer drive her motorized Rascal scooter.

I could wait for management to step in and impound it, of course. It was just a matter of time. But that would be humiliating for her, like being called to the principal's office and reprimanded. No, *I* had to handle this! She was *my* mother, after all!

Her phone rang again. No answer.

I don't know why I was worried. The evidence was on my side. My limp, for instance, from when she had driven her scooter over my foot three days earlier. And the large hole in her foyer wall.

The other residents would thank me, that's for sure. She had been terrorizing them for nearly a year now. They scattered like cockroaches in sunlight when they saw Mom's scooter bearing down on them in the hallways. It was almost comical seeing their reaction the day the elevator door opened and, before we could get on, the few passengers inside took one look at Mom in her scooter and rushed through the door as though they were heading for free-card night at Bingo.

Yesterday had been the final straw. I shuddered when I thought about it. I was having lunch with my mother in the crowded dining room.

"Look Mom, there are two spaces over there," I said, pointing to a round table for eight. We greeted the other six diners and proceeded to take our places. As Mom shifted into *park*, her scooter inched beneath the edge of the table, somehow sliding the gear into forward.

Seeing Mom's Rascal scooter charge ahead, pushing the table with six screaming seniors backwards across the dining room floor and into the tables beyond, was a sight I will not soon forget.

Nobody was hurt, but, sadly, old people are not famous for a sense of humor. And their sense of adventure is right up there with their desire for a Mohawk and a gold nose ring. Naturally, management got wind of the disaster.

⚾ ⚾ ⚾ ⚾

With each ring of Mom's telephone, my heart beat faster. *What now?* I worried, picturing my mother in some new predicament in her apartment. After the fourth ring, she finally picked up.

"Mom?"

"I can't talk to you now, honey. The firemen are still here. I'll call you back when the smoke clears." This is quite possibly the worst response a daughter can hear from her ninety-one-year-old mother.

I dropped the phone and made a beeline for my car. Luckily, my limp was much improved, and in no time, I was on the road and headed to the home, dreading what awaited me. It seemed like just yesterday that I was sixteen and she was handing me the keys to the family car. And today, I had to ask her for the key to her scooter.

The Sunday paper was strewn about Mom's apartment, and the acrid odor of smoke hung in the air. On the kitchen counter, a charcoaled cake clung to the outside of a black pan, and batter was burned to the bottom of the oven.

"Are you all right, Mom? I thought we agreed that you were not going to cook anymore. You do not need to cook!"

"I don't understand it. I've made that cake a hundred times," she said, shaking her head sadly.

I blinked back tears and put on my cheerful face. "Did you

forget it's Sunday? I'll straighten up while you get ready for chapel."

As soon as she left the room, I removed the fuse for the stove and hid it high atop a kitchen cabinet. I opened some windows and, as I gathered up the newspapers, Mom stuck her head around the corner.

"At least I didn't set off the sprinklers like the woman across the hall. She flooded her apartment, and all the furniture had to be moved into the hallway!"

As I took the nearly new wheelchair from the closet, she said, "I wish I could have offered those nice young firemen a piece of my hot milk pound cake."

There was a relaxed sense of calm as I pushed Mom through the long corridors. It was probably the slowest trip she'd made to the chapel since getting her Rascal motorized scooter a year ago. I wanted to say, "Now isn't this civilized, seeing your neighbors' smiling faces instead of their backs as they scramble for the exits?" I thought better of it.

When we arrived at the chapel, I slipped the church offering into Mom's hand, remembering all the nickels and quarters she had slipped into mine so many years ago.

"I'm surprised church isn't over," she said with a twinkle in her eye. "I thought we'd never get here."

Mom was back—at least for now. We could talk about her scooter later.

A Whole New Ballgame: The Most Exciting Day of Mom's Life

By the time a person reaches ninety, the most exciting days of her life are in the past—or so one would expect. When it came to sitting back and watching the world go by, though, my mother, as they say, didn't get the memo.

The ebb and flow of baseball in our lives was like the stream that ran through the fields, overflowing the banks during the Orioles' glory days when they won the American League pennant and slowing to a trickle during those losing seasons Mom described as "rebuilding years," when our hopes hung on promising young prospects in the farm system. The years the Orioles won the World Series, we were swept along in the flood of my mother's mania.

Mom relished the compliments on her new Orioles t-shirt at Oak Crest Village's 2003 Maryland Day celebration. Afterwards, I brought her home with me for an overnight visit.

"I have to change first," she said, as we headed back to her apartment. "It won't take but a minute. I'm all packed."

"Just wear the Orioles shirt," I said. "It looks good."

"No," she said, wrinkling her nose. "Orange isn't really my color."

Following dinner, we tuned in to the Orioles game, the first series of the new season.

"We're playing the Cleveland Indians tonight," she said. "A fresh start. I'm sure we'll do better than last season." Watching a game with Mom was still fun, even if we didn't share her passion.

"I'm going to run to the lavatory now so I won't miss anything," she said. And that's when it happened. A thud, a cry, and Mom lying on the hall floor in pain.

"I think I've broken my hip," she said, while John dialed 911. "Help me over to the sofa so I can watch the game while we wait for the ambulance."

"What? No way, Mom, you'll be in too much pain if we move you."

"I don't care. I want to see the game," she insisted.

And so, in spite of the pain, my mother watched the game until she was carried to the ambulance on a stretcher.

At the hospital, doctors installed a pacemaker and scheduled the risky surgery for her broken hip. On a TV at the foot of her bed, the first pitch of an afternoon game had just been thrown when they came for her.

"I want to hear all about the game afterwards—if I'm still around," she said as I kissed her forehead. "We're tied for third."

Seconds later, my mother rode to surgery on a noisy gurney with one concern—the Orioles' American League standing.

Hours later an ICU nurse removed a breathing tube and Mom's eyes slowly opened. She squeezed my hand and, to the accompaniment of blinking and beeping high-tech machines, I leaned close, struggling to hear. I expected questions about the surgery. *Was it successful? How long until I can walk? When can I go home?*

I should have known better.

"Well, I'm still alive," she whispered in a faint, raspy voice. "Did the Orioles win?"

Rehab was painfully slow with the quiet, withdrawn patient bearing little resemblance to the mother I knew. I had never seen her ill. Although when I was sick as a child, with scarlet fever and later pneumonia, Mom had stayed at my side, reminiscing about her own childhood illnesses.

"I was twelve the first time I almost died," she had told me. Of course, I had heard this story a few times, but I didn't mind. "I had appendicitis, and Dr. Cockrell carried me down to the docks and aboard the Piankatank steamboat. It was dark and scary with eerie foghorns, but he sat with me all night until we got to the hospital in Baltimore. Mama couldn't come because she'd just had my baby sister." Her finish was filled with drama.

"They told me at the hospital, 'Thelma, your appendix burst, and you are lucky to be alive!'"

To a sick child, Mom's stories had been comforting. Not just because she knew how to tell a story, but because they always had a happy ending.

"The second time I almost died, I drank water from a contaminated well and got typhoid fever," she said. "I was delirious with a high fever. Mama cried every day and put my burial outfit in the bottom dresser drawer. And then, one day I sat straight up in bed and asked for some Coca-Cola. And Mama said, 'Praise the Lord!'"

I was determined to be there for my mother the way she had always been there for me. I wanted her to know that this story, too, would have a happy ending.

⚾ ⚾ ⚾ ⚾

"We'll be working with Miss Thelma twice a day," the physical therapist told me. "She needs all the encouragement we can give her."

Mom's only interest during those long spring days was baseball. Even then, her response was oddly subdued.

I longed to hear, "Just hit the damn ball!" one more time. And then came the devastating news.

"Mrs. Knobel has made no progress at all. If she doesn't start making an effort, we'll have to discontinue her physical therapy. She'll spend the rest of her days in a bed or wheelchair."

In desperation, I sat at my computer and wrote a letter to the Baltimore Orioles front office describing an elderly fan's years of unwavering devotion. Every word was true.

"Even when the Orioles fell behind or played late night games on the West Coast, Thelma listened until the final out."

I told them how she had insisted on watching the Orioles while in pain and waiting for the ambulance and how her primary concern following surgery was the outcome of the game.

"If only you could send a card signed by the players, it might give her the will to go on," I said.

Two days later the call came—a cheerful, upbeat young woman. "Would Mrs. Knobel be able to attend an Orioles game at Camden Yards in July?"

I was speechless.

"If so, we would like for her to throw out the opening pitch. Do you think she'd be interested?"

Interested, indeed! When I found my voice, I explained my mother's mobility issues.

"Oh, we're willing to work around her schedule," the young woman said. "Whenever she's ready."

That afternoon as I was leaving for Oak Crest, a baseball signed by Mike Flanagan, a Cy Young winner and Orioles GM, arrived in the mail. I found Mom in the cafeteria resting her head in her hand and pushing food around her plate like a child.

"Look what I have," I said, placing the ball on the table. "It's for you."

She stared at it.

"Mom, the Orioles have invited you to throw out the opening pitch at a game in Camden Yards."

She looked up at me, her eyes vacant, and my spirits plummeted. I prayed that it wasn't too late. If only she would sit up and ask for some Coca-Cola.

"Mom, did you hear me?" I said a little louder. "The Baltimore Orioles have invited you to Camden Yards to throw out the opening pitch in July! Be excited!"

She picked up the ball and turned it over and over in her hands. Suddenly, there was a sparkle in her eyes I hadn't seen in the months since Dad died. Her eyebrows shot up.

"Well, I hope they don't expect me to sing the national anthem!"

I laughed, although I wasn't sure if she was making a joke or setting some ground rules.

When I wheeled her down the hall to PT that afternoon, she made an announcement.

"We have work to do! I have to be able to walk to the pitcher's mound at Camden Yards in July!"

⚾ ⚾ ⚾ ⚾

In July 2003, our family accompanied my ninety-year-old mother to Camden Yards. Orioles owner Peter Angelos surprised us with an offer to use his private box. In the dugout before the game, players and staff came to chat and sign autographs. Mom even discussed strategy with coaches Elrod

Hendricks and Rick Dempsey, giving them some valuable advice for the pitching staff.

During a tour of the press box where we were introduced to the play-by-play announcers whose voices she had known so intimately. Mom was strangely mute, as if in the presence of greatness.

On the field, amidst the hustle and bustle of batting practice, came the moment that brought a broad smile to Mom's face and confirmed to me that her new pacemaker was indeed working. Cy Young Award winner and Hall of Fame pitcher Jim Palmer walked up to my mother, knelt beside her wheelchair, and talked baseball with his biggest fan. Afterward, as he walked away, Mom remembered something and waved her hand through the air.

"Oh Jim! Jim!" she called. He turned around, walked back to my mother, and with a patient smile, knelt once more beside the wheelchair.

"Yes, Miss Thelma."

I could have kissed him, quite literally!

"I wanted to tell you how much I enjoyed your article in *The Baltimore Sun* this morning. I agreed with all of it!"

"Thank you, Miss Thelma. It had to be said, and I meant every word." And then, the great Jim Palmer shook my mother's hand, ever so gently.

Minutes later, two ball girls assisted the Orioles' most loyal supporter as she limped onto the field. To a standing ovation from tens of thousands, Mom stood on hallowed ground and delivered the underarm pitch she had been practicing in PT. It bounced to the pitcher who snagged it twenty-five feet away.

Moments later, with Mom once again seated in her wheelchair, our guide presented her with a shiny white plastic bag with an Orioles logo on the front.

"Here you go, Mrs. Knobel, a little souvenir of your visit to

Camden Yards. And now we need to let these men play some baseball," she said.

It wasn't until the third inning that Mom remembered the bag and took it from the wheelchair pocket. It contained a book, the baseball she had thrown, and one other item.

"Oh, isn't this nice," she said, holding up the orange t-shirt with "Orioles" written across the front.

My gasp was heard rows away, as I remembered a similar shirt and Mom's unforgettable performance in that busy aisle at Macy's.

"Why don't you just keep this, Peggy," she said with a twinkle in her eye. "I already have one. Besides, orange isn't really my color."

I accepted the shirt, a reminder of my mother's unbridled passion for the Baltimore Orioles.

As a matter of fact, I still have it—and I expect I always will.

Epilogue

Thanks to the Orioles, Thelma Knobel was propelled to instant celebrity status at Oak Crest. Her picture hung in elevators and on bulletin boards, and her story was in *Guideposts* magazine as well as *The Baltimore Sun*.

In a TV interview, she summed up her July visit to Camden Yards in one sentence: "It was the most exciting day of my life!"

I have no doubt that she had spoken the truth.

Family Remembrances

"After I got married and set up housekeeping, Mother and Dad would visit. While I was busy in the kitchen or tending to the children, Mom was also busy—rearranging the furniture or redecorating my tabletops. She always knew what looked best. If I ever doubted her love for me, I only had to remember the tears streaming down her cheeks as she and Dad dropped me off at the freshman dorm that first day of college.

~ Janet Knobel Jones, Daughter

"Nana's house had a special odor—a combination of cleaning products and something baking in the oven. During baseball games, she had the TV on without sound and the radio blaring beside her. She was either clapping her hands or yelling at the ump for making a bad call. Getting my shirt tucked in, my hair brushed, or my hands washed was a small price to pay for cookies and entertainment."

~ Philip Daniel Rowe, Grandson

"I had the great fortune to grow up with loving grandparents who lived just a short walk across the yard. In a sense, I had two homes. To my childhood mind, the love of our grandparents transcended the mundane devotion of mere parental love. Mom and Dad would correct us, and 'do what was best for us' while Nana and Pop would give of themselves for the joy of a smile and a hug. That meant meatloaf and chores at one end of the yard, and cookies and TV at the other. No contest! From the vantage of middle age, I see that my grandparents were special in the way that all loving grandparents are special. A testament to the power of family— never missing an opportunity to share their love—our one true legacy."

~ Scott Carl Rowe, Grandson

"Visiting Nana and Poppie for extended summer vacations meant a trip to Memorial Stadium to see a ballgame. Sitting beside the Orioles' biggest fan was exciting stuff for a little leaguer. It was always the highlight of my summer."

~ Gary Kevin Jones, Grandson

"I enjoyed ballgames with Nana, but even more, I loved visiting Fleeton, Virginia, when she was there. We shared a love of crabbing. I can still see her wading through the sea grass with a dip net and a rope tied around her waist, towing an inner tube with a bucket for soft crabs."—Stephen Morris Jones, Grandson

"Aunt Thelma was my hero and my role model. She showed me that a woman could have a career and be independent if she chose. Whenever there was a problem, Aunt Thelma had a way of stepping in and making things right."

~ Nancy Kube Fine, Niece

Discussion Questions for Book Clubs by Marjie Rowe

We meet an older Thelma in the opening scene. What did you think of her? Did your first impression of her remain throughout the book or did it change?

You have met many of Peggy's relatives. Whom would you like to meet and get to know better? Why?

What was the most compelling memory shared by Peggy in the book? Can you relate to it in a personal way?

What personal parallels can you make between the author's upbringing and your own? Is it similar or different?

This book gives us a look at being raised in the 20th century. How is family life and childrearing the same now in the 21st century?

How is it different?

Why do you think Thelma was so enamored with the Orioles? Discuss what Peggy maintains as her "two very different mothers living in the same body."

The author compares herself to her mother throughout the book. Do you think they were truly so very different?

Discuss the family values portrayed in the book. Do they still hold true for today?

Would you want Thelma or Peggy for a mother? Why or why not?

How does the author's use of humor enhance the readers' empathy for the characters in the book?

What do you think was the most humorous memory shared in the book? Why?

What makes reading about Peggy and Thelma so appealing?